Praise for

How (not) to Save the World

"Hosanna has discovered the blueprint this generation needs to know how to show God's love in this day and age. Her deep love for those far from God is evident in how she writes, speaks, and lives. With tender authority and inspiring practicality, Hosanna will show you how to fight for those you love, step into your calling, and say yes to Jesus with all your heart. Beautiful and brave, Hosanna is a voice for this moment and makes me excited about the future that stretches before us."

—LISA BEVERE

NEW YORK TIMES BESTSELLING AUTHOR AND
COFOUNDER OF MESSENGER INTERNATIONAL

"We all know we aren't the Savior, yet we carry the weight of wanting others to experience Jesus like we do. But how can we authentically have these conversations without getting tripped up on all our differences and coming across as weird or pushy? Hosanna has learned the secret of cultivating real connection by simply stepping into the everyday world of people she loves and fighting for their relationship. In *How (Not) to Save the World*, Hosanna teaches us that the most effective person Jesus wants to use to reach the people you love is in fact *you*. This message is our tool to not only fight for those we love but fight for the world Jesus loves."

—LYSA TERKEURST

#1 *NEW YORK TIMES* BESTSELLING AUTHOR AND
PRESIDENT OF PROVERBS 31 MINISTRIES

"Hosanna's heart beats for the broken, and her soul chases hard after Jesus. That same heart and soul permeate every word, every line, and every story in *How (Not) to Save the World*. If your heart beats for the people you love, and if your soul longs for our Savior, then this is the guidebook you need in your life today. Get ready for a changed perspective, a changed mission, and changed lives."

—JUD AND LORI WILHITE
SENIOR PASTOR AT CENTRAL CHURCH IN LAS VEGAS
FOUNDER OF LEADING AND LOVING IT

"My friend Hosanna radiates the love of Jesus. She has lived a compelling life and wants to help you do the same. In *How (Not) to Save the World*, her vulnerability will inspire you, her wisdom will inform you, and her love of Jesus will transform you."

—DR. DERWIN L. GRAY
COFOUNDER AND LEAD PASTOR OF TRANSFORMATION
CHURCH AND AUTHOR OF *GOD, DO YOU HEAR ME?*

"It can be easy to feel locked up when it comes to sharing God's love with others. We can let so many lies keep us back from trusting God, taking risks, and stepping out in faith to be who God's called us to be and to love others like God's called us to love. In *How (Not) to Save the World*, Hosanna helps us see how we can be confident in living our story, sharing it, and ultimately living our lives for His glory in a winsome way. This book will take your life to the next level!"

—JENNIE LUSKO
COPASTOR OF FRESH LIFE CHURCH AND BESTSELLING
AUTHOR OF *THE FIGHT TO FLOURISH*

"Hosanna is one of the freshest voices and hearts in our culture. Her vulnerability and passion are contagious. I love this book!"

—SHEILA WALSH
AUTHOR OF *HOLDING ON WHEN YOU WANT TO LET GO*

"I have loved Hosanna since the moment I met her. I was first struck by her wisdom and communication skills and second by the way she truly desires to make much of Jesus in her life. Wisdom plus communication skills without the love of Jesus are not impressive. Hosanna is impressive—because of Jesus. She oozes the love of Jesus to anyone who is around her. I have been impacted by her story and passion for Jesus, and I'm very confident that you will feel the same when you finish the final page of this book."

—JAMIE IVEY
BESTSELLING AUTHOR, PODCAST HOST, YOUTUBE HOST

"At a moment in time when the church's reputation is faltering (to say the least), *How (Not) to Save the World* is the lifeline we desperately need. Hosanna guides us back to the basics of living the type of love-drenched, transparent life necessary for carrying out Jesus' ultimate mission. Will it cost us? Yes. Will it be worth it? Absolutely."

—DR. ANITA PHILLIPS
THERAPIST AND HOST, *IN THE LIGHT* PODCAST

"Through trial and error, Hosanna has done the hard work of learning what works and, more importantly, what doesn't work about spreading the good news of Jesus Christ. Her powerful book not only outlines applicable lessons that will help all of us but is also a beautiful tribute to her father, his ministry, and his impact on her life."

—JOHNNY AND JENI BAKER
PASTOR AND AUTHOR OF *THE ROAD TO FREEDOM*
GLOBAL COEXECUTIVE DIRECTORS OF CELEBRATE RECOVERY

"In this beautiful offering, *How (Not) to Save the World*, Hosanna offers the truth right up front: Jesus has already saved the world! Thank You, Jesus. He does, however, long for our 'yes' to His purpose and plans for us to come alongside His beautiful plans to tell all people. This book is an invitation to your place in the beautiful story. Hosanna's inspiring 'yes' opens the door for us all."

—SHELLEY GIGLIO
COFOUNDER OF PASSION CONFERENCES AND PASSION CITY CHURCH

"Having served together and walked in ministry with Hosanna for several years, I can tell you she lives what she speaks and writes. In *How (Not) to Save the World*, her genuine love for people and passion for the Jesus mission are on full display. Like her speaking, this book will have you laughing and learning and will leave you more motivated and better equipped to share the good news of Jesus with those where you live, work, and play. I highly recommend it."

—JAMES GROGAN
SENIOR PASTOR OF THE COMMUNITY CHURCH MOVEMENT
AND LEAD PASTOR OF EASTLAKE CHURCH

How (not) to Save the World

How (not) to Save the World

THE TRUTH ABOUT REVEALING GOD'S LOVE TO THE PEOPLE RIGHT NEXT TO *You*

HOSANNA WONG

W PUBLISHING GROUP

AN IMPRINT OF THOMAS NELSON

Published in Nashville, Tennessee, by W Publishing, an imprint of Thomas Nelson.

Published in association with literary agent Jenni Burke of Illuminate Literary Agency, www.illluminateliterary.com.

Thomas Nelson titles may be purchased in bulk for educational, business, fund-raising, or sales promotional use. For information, please email SpecialMarkets@ThomasNelson.com.

Unless otherwise noted, Scripture quotations are taken from The Voice™. Copyright © 2012 by Ecclesia Bible Society. Used by permission. All rights reserved.

Scripture quotations marked CEB are taken from the Common English Bible. Copyright © 2011 Common English Bible. Scripture quotations marked CEV are taken from the Contemporary English Version. Copyright © 1991, 1992, 1995 by American Bible Society. Used by permission. Scripture quotations marked CSB are taken from the Christian Standard Bible®. Copyright © 2017 by Holman Bible Publishers. Used by permission. Christian Standard Bible® and CSB® are federally registered trademarks of Holman Bible Publishers. Scripture quotations marked GW are taken from God's Word®. © 1995, 2003, 2013, 2014, 2019, 2020 by God's Word to the Nations Mission Society. Used by permission. Scripture quotations marked MSG are taken from THE MESSAGE. Copyright © 1993, 2002, 2018 by Eugene H. Peterson. Used by permission of NavPress. All rights reserved. Represented by Tyndale House Publishers, a Division of Tyndale House Ministries. Scripture quotations marked NASB are taken from the New American Standard Bible® (NASB®). Copyright © 1960, 1971, 1977, 1995, 2020 by The Lockman Foundation. Used by permission. All rights reserved. www.lockman.org. Scripture quotations marked NIV are taken from the Holy Bible, New International Version®, NIV®. Copyright © 1973, 1978, 1984, 2011 by Biblica, Inc.® Used by permission of Zondervan. All rights reserved worldwide. www.zondervan.com. The "NIV" and "New International Version" are trademarks registered in the United States Patent and Trademark Office by Biblica, Inc.® Scripture quotations marked NKJV are taken from the New King James Version®. Copyright © 1982 by Thomas Nelson. Used by permission. All rights reserved. Scripture quotations marked NLT are taken from the Holy Bible, New Living Translation. Copyright © 1996, 2004, 2015 by Tyndale House Foundation. Used by permission of Tyndale House Ministries, Carol Stream, Illinois 60188. All rights reserved. Scripture quotations marked RSV are taken from Revised Standard Version of the Bible. Copyright © 1946, 1952, and 1971 National Council of the Churches of Christ in the United States of America. Used by permission. All rights reserved.

ISBN 978-0-7852-4302-1 (SC)
ISBN 978-0-7852-4347-2 (audiobook)
ISBN 978-0-7852-4333-5 (eBook)

Library of Congress Control Number: 2021934638

Printed in the United States of America
21 22 23 24 25 LSC 10 9 8 7 6 5 4 3 2 1

To my dad.
Thank you for how fearlessly you lived and how deeply
you loved. Thank you for teaching me how to talk about
Jesus, how to fight for those far from God, and how to
shoot free throws. I'm still trying my best at all three.
You're my hero. I'll love you forever. I'll see you soon.
Love, your little girl

Contents

How (not) to Save the World

Contents

Foreword

"Mummy, do you think God can use someone like me? I'm not like you. I don't have a big, dramatic past or exciting salvation story. My life is pretty normal. Is it possible to make a difference in the world if I don't have a powerful testimony?"

When my eldest daughter, Catherine, asked me that question, it stopped me in my tracks. She was in her mid-teens and had just returned from a week of church camp where a compelling youth evangelist shared his amazing story of being lost and found, of being strung out on drugs, addicted to alcohol, and wandering in the darkness before stepping into the light of Christ—all in hopes of inspiring teens like Catherine to give their lives to Jesus.

As an evangelist for more than three decades, I have been the speaker at camps like this one countless times, so I completely understood the purpose of his message. But it left Catherine with the idea that because she *didn't* have a testimony that included brokenness, filled with pain and addiction, she didn't have much to say about her Christian faith. It left her feeling like she didn't have, and couldn't be, an effective witness.

It was sobering for me, as a mother, to realize that I had also missed communicating to my own daughter the true meaning of the gospel. Like so many others, she has been in church all her life but still does not really understand the heart of the good news. I had to share with her the truth of the gospel because what she was hearing, in so many words, was that if you had a really bad past, you needed Jesus. But if you didn't have a really bad past, you didn't need Him—or at least not as much.

Nothing could be further from the truth, but that was the point: she didn't fully understand the truth.

As I began gathering my thoughts to help her realize her own incredible testimony, it occurred to me that before any of us can grasp the good news, first we need to comprehend the bad news. Before I was alive in Christ, I was dead. We all were.

As Catherine and I began to talk, I explained how Jesus came to make dead people alive, not bad people good. We were all dead on arrival, and Jesus came to give us new life. And yet we seem to easily connect the idea that "I did a bad thing, so I need forgiveness" rather than "There is none righteous, no, not one," including myself— whether I did a bad thing or not (Rom. 3:10 NKJV).

I walked Catherine through the Word—the only source of absolute truth—to help her understand the real meaning of the gospel. To help her realize she has a story to tell because the gospel isn't about our behavior or works; it's about Jesus' grace—for by grace we have been saved through faith, not through ourselves or by our own works (Eph. 2:8). Grace is a gift from God. Faith is about what He did for us. About His love for us.

Sharing this life-changing truth with the people right next to us is what my dear friend Hosanna has laid out beautifully in her book *How (not) to Save the World*. Ever so thoughtfully, she takes the last command Jesus gave us, the one He took the time to tell us on His way to heaven, and shows us how to actually follow it. Jesus said,

"Go, therefore, and make disciples of all nations, baptizing them in the name of the Father and of the Son and of the Holy Spirit" (Matt. 28:19 csb).

Through page after page of encouragement, Hosanna helps us all understand that Jesus' first invitation is for us to know Him and then to partner with Him on His mission for others to know Him. To go and make disciples. She helps us understand that we have been created and equipped for that very mission, in our lifetimes, with our own personalities, passions, and positions, including the ways we feel inadequate.

By tackling the lies we often believe—lies that hold us back from being real and being ourselves—she moves us forward to partner with God on His mission to save the world. She defuses the pressure, the guilt, the defeat, and the misguided ideas we have believed, then helps us overcome our fear of failing and the fear of how people might respond. She understands that what we need and want to say has been in us all along, and we weren't meant to do it alone.

By sharing her own experiences, Hosanna helps us understand that we *can* tell our friends. We *can* let His joy seep through our lives. By you and me extending invitations, having conversations, and sharing our stories, we *can* reveal God's love to the people right next to us.

As a fellow Jesus-follower, an evangelist, and a mother, I couldn't be happier knowing Hosanna is helping yet another generation understand God's mission, the most important mission in the world.

The power in this book is that Hosanna lives the message she shares on these pages. She writes so poignantly, "At the end of our lives, when we see Jesus face-to-face, we will not be held accountable for what others told us to do and not do. We will only be held accountable for what God said to do and if we did it."

Jesus told us to go and make disciples.

Let Hosanna inspire you the way she has inspired me—to be yourself and allow God to use you to help fulfill His mission to save the world.

—CHRISTINE CAINE
Founder, A21 and Propel Women

Confessions from an Expert

Ten years ago I packed my life into suitcases and started traveling the country to share the story of Jesus through spoken-word poetry. I didn't have a plan or a home address and wouldn't for years. And there were a whole lot of things I wasn't sure of.

I wasn't sure how to love the people right next to me.

I wasn't sure how to step into what God was calling me to do.

I wasn't sure how to embrace community or what I even thought about the church.

Put simply, I wasn't sure how to actually make Jesus known to real people. Living on mission for God? I wasn't sure what that even meant.

So I fumbled through it—a lot. And I often got things oh so very wrong.

That's why I've written this book.

It turns out, I'm an expert on how (not) to save the world. I've believed so many lies about myself, my purpose and calling, and the community of the church.

These lies have *not* led me to confidence in who I am created to be or closeness to the One who created me. They have not led me to greater purpose, greater peace, or greater impact. Instead, they have left me feeling exhausted, depleted, guilty, prideful, and at times, apathetic, giving up altogether on Jesus' call to show the world His love.

And, without intending to, I've pushed away those I love. I've given more monologues than I've participated in dialogues. I've cared about being right more than caring for a relationship. I've wanted to pass on the story of Jesus but haven't felt smart enough, skilled enough, or spiritual enough for such an important task. I've wanted to say yes and step into what I've felt God calling me to do, but fears of failing have caused me to step back.

Through faithfully studying God's Word and fumbling through my own flawed progress, I've discovered something better: the truth about revealing God's love to the people right next to us.

This is the book I needed ten years ago—the book that would have told me what I want to tell you now:

- You can fight for the people you love.
- You can say yes to what God is calling you to do without fear of failing.
- The church is better when you're in it, and His community unified together is His favorite plan to help a hurting world.
- The most important mission in the world will absolutely require your participation. You've been equipped for it. You've been created for it. You've been handmade and handpicked for it.
- The details of your life's story—who you are, what you love, and all that you've been through—are exactly what God wants to use for this exact moment in time.

It turns out, we *can* naturally share the truth about Jesus in our everyday lives. We *can* let those around us know how valuable they are. We *can* fight for those we love and a world Jesus loves. There *is* a way for every person we know to realize how loved they are by God.

I've written this book so that every chapter exposes a lie that has held us back from showing God's love. We have a choice: believe the lies or live out the truth.

The truth is better.

People need to know how much God loves them. Somebody needs to tell them. And it's us. It's me and you. We're the ones God has picked for this very purpose. Our details and our experiences have uniquely equipped us to show people who God is within our lifetimes.

Let's not wait another second. Join me in discovering the simple truths that can set us free and set those we love free as well.

Ready?

Together, let's go.

How (not) to Save the World

#1 | Rely on Your Own Power

The first time I witnessed a murder I was nine years old.

I was sitting on crimson brick steps that were growing ever warmer from the blazing summer sun, next to my three-year-old brother, Elijah, in a run-down public park in the inner city of San Francisco. I grew up in this park. One side was covered with patches of browning grass, the other with climbing brick steps, hidden by layers of faded graffiti. Though the park lacked traditional swings and slides, our imaginations created colorful worlds, making this playground our mansion in the sky, our castle in a distant land.

When I was still in my mom's belly, my parents founded an outreach to those living on the streets in the Tenderloin district of San Francisco. Most of my childhood was spent in this park with my family, holding church services and Bible studies multiple days a week, handing out thousands of lunches and items of clothing, playing chess with our friends, and watching basketball games. Both sides of the park were occupied by hundreds without homes, battling addiction, recently released from prison, or running away from . . . something. To many, this was a dangerous destination where needles slayed arms like knights slayed dragons, where runaways and misfits strayed if they had no place to go. To us, this was where we created a family. This was where we had church.

Gang members of all ages and backgrounds came to our services, and, sure, *sometimes* violent brawls would break out, but no fear, we all quickly became good friends with the local police officers stationed across the street. Fights were broken up, and we'd continue with services. That sort of week was typical. (Later in life I learned that when people asked me if I grew up in church and I responded yes, it didn't mean the *exact* same thing to everyone as it did to me. *Fair enough.*)

When screeches of laughter suddenly rang out from the park's beat-up basketball court, many of us would gather to watch the latest scrimmage, squeezing in on the sides of the cement court or surrounding steps, all delicately painted with pigeon droppings. Gated by tall, Emerald City–like fences but with chipped black paint and explicit words carved into them (much different from Dorothy's dream utopia), there was nothing Oz, fake, or hidden about this park on the corner of Jones and Eddy Streets. Still, for me, there was no place like home.

The trouble that sad, scorching day started when hateful insults echoed between the city buildings towering over me and Elijah. Before long, the two groups of people shouting faced off directly in front of us. Their words were some of the worst that humans could come up with—some words I had never heard before. The two groups hated each other. They hated each other with such intensity for their differences that they were both prepared to kill because of it.

The first knife-pulling rearranged the air, and I failed to shield my brother's eyes in time. My body froze as I watched the violence unfold just feet away from us. Stab. Slice. *Stop!* I wanted to scream. But I didn't. I could not process what I was seeing. *Am I allowed to be here? Do they see us sitting here?* Another knife appeared. Stab. Slice. Swarm. A group of people surrounded the scene, and I couldn't make out what was happening except that small fights were breaking out among the bigger fight. That part is a hurried blur. It was not like the fight scenes in movies. There was no music. There were no camera angles helping me know where to look. It was confusing. It was loud. Fast. Then the crowd backed off. Two men seemed to be hugging. But they weren't. As one man released his embrace, another fell to the cracked concrete with a knife lodged in his chest. The various groups jumped the chipped fence and fled the park. I couldn't tell who'd won . . . it did not feel like there were winners that day. Bodies lay limp on the ground. I couldn't see how many. As I stepped closer to see who was still fighting for their life and who was already gone, the police ran in, crowds blocked my view, and an ambulance took someone away.

Our utopia would never be the same.

Looking down at my worn-out sneakers, grass stained from the days I'd run freely in this park I loved so much, there was a queasy feeling in my stomach that I had accidentally just grown up a little. I knew I had seen something I was not supposed to see. I looked at my little brother and felt a feeling I had never felt before.

Guilt.

This was the first moment I remember feeling like I was supposed to save somebody, but I didn't.

I replayed the event in my mind for weeks after, wishing I could go back and do something different. A hurricane of should-haves swarmed within my mind and took over my thoughts.

I should have picked up my brother and run away.

I should have screamed for help.

I should have sprinted toward the fight and tried to break it up.

Maybe a little girl screaming and jumping up and down would have stopped everyone in their tracks. I should have at least tried! I should have done more.

The early inner workings of guilt were planted within my frail nine-year-old heart. They continued to sprout like weeds. I signed up for as many community outreaches as possible, but our neighborhood's needs never seemed to lessen. I tried to invite my basketball teammates to church with me, but none of them accepted the invitation. I tried to do more, save more, and save better, and instead, the disappointing results left me insecure and angry.

- Angry at the people in my life I couldn't help.
- Angry at the circumstances I couldn't change.
- Angry at myself for being powerless to save people.

From a young age I felt helpless amid blaringly obvious brokenness. The crooked streets I grew up on never seemed to straighten out, and though I strived to be increasingly braver and more diligent in my part to make a difference, I could not shake the haunting feeling of how meaningless my small actions were in the grand scheme of things. I wanted to save the world. But how?

WE NEED A SAVIOR

No matter how or where we grew up, many of us know what it feels like to have seen things we were not sure we should have seen and learned things we were not prepared to know. Over the years, we've grown overwhelmed and disheartened by the insurmountable needs around us. We have witnessed hearts broken within our own homes, hateful words echoing not amid downtown buildings but among the walls of our houses. We've seen the people right next to us battle with loss, hopelessness, and pain. And we've seen people far from us experience it too. We've seen murder on our televisions or in videos replayed on our cell phones. We have been flooded with never-ending slideshows of famines, global pandemics, and violence in our own streets and across the world. We've seen towers fall. We've watched bombs go off during races. We've seen the horrific numbers of humans who have been abducted, abused, and sold like property and the faces of precious children without parents. We've heard the sound of a clenched fist connecting with a face in a fight—without cinematic sound effects, a true knuckle-to-cheekbone thump is far less entertaining. This is not like the movies. This is not fun. And there are no end credits in sight.

We are all painfully aware that our loved ones are hurting. We are terrifyingly in tune to the fact that our world is in dire need of saving. This is not a book about how much pain our world is in. Instead, this is a book for people who want to be a part of the solution.

We want to save the world. But how?

How do we save when we feel powerless?

How do we save when our solutions have missed the mark?

How do we save when we feel frozen in fears of failing?

I want to remind you or perhaps let you in on this freeing truth for the first time:

- Jesus is the Savior.
- Jesus has the power to save.
- We do not.

At an early age I believed the lie that as a Jesus-follower it was now my duty to save everyone around me. *If I didn't, then I was falling short.*

The truth is freeing.

It is not our job to save.

Jesus is the Savior of the world. That task was His calling. Not ours. You and I actually don't have the power to do it. That's why Jesus came to do it. And great news: He *already* saved the world.

E

X

H

A

L

E.

Thank God. *(Literally.)*

We were not created to bear the weight of everyone's salvation on our shoulders. This leads to an unhealthy amount of pressure, resulting in ungodly feelings of guilt and insecurity, especially when we've tried our best to do something and still haven't seen results.

- We've tried to talk with our family members about Jesus but couldn't find the right words or the right moment.
- We've tried to start a small group to mentor young couples, but our doorbell never rang, and our homemade meals grew cold.
- We've tried to help our nephew get into a recovery program, but we waited for him in the parking lot for hours and he never showed.

When we see *ourselves* as saviors, we can start finding our identity in the outcome of what we do, at times seeing ourselves as greater than we are—basking in the success of our achievements and overly self-assured in our savior-like abilities.

At other times we see ourselves as less than we are—feeling disproportionately insecure, empty, and meaningless when we feel like we've failed at an important task. We can begin hurting ourselves and others from the all-consuming unrest, burning ourselves out by the insistent striving, or finding ourselves frozen from doing *anything* due to fear of failing.

Relying on our own power will not help us, those we love, or a world far from God. We need someone more powerful than us.

SATURDAY-MORNING SUPERHEROES

As a little girl I would leap out of bed early on Saturday mornings to watch the latest episode of *Batman*. I would press up against the cold glass screen of our small, static television and get lost in the inner workings of Gotham City as the heroic duo combatted the evil schemes of Two-Face, the Riddler, Catwoman, and the best villain of all time, the Joker. (Not up for debate.)

There's something exhilarating about watching the good guys overtake the bad guys, coming out of nowhere in the exact moment of dire need with impressive skills and explosive weapons in the sky—even in clearly uncomfortable tights. (Dear *Project Runway*, please do a hero-makeover challenge *soon*. As the great poet Beyoncé once said, "Let me upgrade you."[1]) When the *Justice League* cartoon began, and it featured a whole host of heroes—including the one and only truth-lassoing Wonder Woman—I was sold. Girls could be heroes too? I was all in. I wanted to know about superheroes. I wanted to *be* a superhero.

The religious people of Jesus' day were also looking for a hero. Just as it is to us, the brokenness of the world was glaringly obvious to them, and they believed a king, a warrior, was coming to defeat the evil empires, fight off the tyrannical leaders, and forcefully turn over the corrupted governments of the day. Also, hopefully, he would judge and destroy all of those horrible sinners everywhere. They awaited a hero's arrival.

And someone did come. He had more power than they could ever comprehend, and yet He didn't come to take over with forceful power at all.

Instead, they were introduced to a Savior not participating in remarkable battles, showing off His spectacular strength, or lobbying for titles to invoke His impressive status; no, He gave up His status. In a world where we naturally seek glory and applaud those we also find glorious, we surprisingly find that the One who already had all the glory did not aim to be above us but came to be *with* us. The distinguished Savior emptied Himself of His outward splendor and "made himself nothing by taking the very nature of a servant, being made in human likeness" to serve other humans (Phil. 2:7 NIV). He came to hang out with, love, and serve the ones the religious people hoped He'd judge and destroy. *And for the record*, He also came for the judgmental religious people—sinners who were much more eager to point out others' sins than to consider their own. He came to forgive and save them too.

It turns out, in our quest to be Savior-like, to be Christlike, and to live like Jesus would, servanthood is the example we're given. The call to be like Jesus is not a call to save. It is a call to serve. It is not a commission to become greater; it is an invitation to become less. There is no mandate on you to save the world. There is a mission for you to love the world Jesus came to save.

The battle for people's lives will not be won in grandiose battles in the sky, with capes flying in the wind, with front-page who's-stronger-than-who battles and egotistical showboating. The battle for people's lives will be won on the ground, loving and serving people, many times privately, in our homes, schools, places of work, on our city streets, and in our everyday lives.

> There is no mandate on you to save the world. There is a mission for you to love the world Jesus came to save.

The pressure to be a hero is off. The guilt of failing to be God is gone. The salvation of your family, your workplace, and your city is not all on you. Jesus is the One who saves lives, who heals marriages, who sets people free from addictions, and who makes the impossible possible. Our power can't compare to His. We are neither the climax of the story nor the main point. Jesus is the subject, and we are the storytellers.

This simple truth liberates me to take more risks without fearing failure. To share with people the wonderful news of what Jesus has done in my life without feeling the pressure of what those results will be. To be myself around coworkers, throw a dinner party and invite people that I might previously have been too embarrassed to invite, start a Bible study and not freak out about how many (or how few) people show up, share my story even if it isn't perfect yet, serve people who may not show gratitude, and share Jesus with people who may never accept Him. I'm free to fumble. I'm free to risk. I'm freer than I've ever imagined.

Phew! What a load off. I was never a very good savior anyway.

THE HERO

There's a story in the Bible of a guy who also thought he had to rely on his own power. Nose in the air, confident of how well he knew the Scriptures, he asked Jesus what he needed to do to *earn* eternal life, hoping to trap Jesus. This well-educated man was fishing to find loopholes in Jesus' theology and form the ultimate pushback to the crazy notion that faith in Jesus was enough for salvation. Jesus responded by asking him what the Scriptures say, and the scholar knowledgeably replied, "Love the Lord your God and love your neighbor."

Jesus simply said to go and do exactly that.

I imagine the man looking at his friends and rolling his eyes as they chuckled, their feet dusted with warm sand filling their sandals and their hearts similarly dirty with pride. Trying to trap Jesus yet again, the man asked, "Who is my neighbor?"

What a bizarre thing to ask. If loving God and loving your neighbor was the way to grab hold of eternal life, why wouldn't he ask Jesus, "*How* can I love God, and *how* can I love my neighbor?" His clarification of *who* is my neighbor shows he was hoping to have an exclusive list. (Self-righteous people love those.) The man questioning Jesus wanted to know the boxes to check. He wanted to replace Jesus' saving grace with a to-do list. He wanted to earn. He wanted to achieve. Like many of us do when we rely on our own power, he wanted to remove the spotlight from what Jesus could do and focus more on what humans could do. And then Jesus told the story of the good Samaritan.

We frequently use this term today to describe someone who does something kind. "That guy brought my Amazon order to my house when it was accidentally delivered to him in another neighborhood! What a good Samaritan!" (A true story of what happened to me yesterday. Thanks, Casey S.! I needed that salsa!) And we've often heard this story as if it's about bad guys (priests and Levites—religious people ignoring and passing by a beat-up and bleeding man on the side of the road) and good guys (the Samaritan who compassionately stopped, took pity on the hurting man, brought him to an inn to be taken care of, and told the innkeeper he'd pay for and provide whatever was necessary for the man's full recovery.)

Jesus finished the story, looked to the self-righteous scholar, and asked, "Who loved their neighbor?" Jews hated Samaritans, so the scholar, refusing to name the helpful person in front of his attentive audience, and more irritated at Jesus than the pebbles in his sandals, quickly said, "The one who showed mercy." ·

Jesus then said, "Go and do likewise" (Luke 10:37 RSV).

There are profound lessons to be found in the story of the good Samaritan for sure. More than we can unpack here. Things like: We don't want to pass by those right in front of us who are hurting. We don't want to be deterred by those who are different from us. We don't want to ignore people's needs. Observing isn't enough. Posting online isn't enough. We need to take notice *and* take action.

That is all true, and that sermon will preach! But there's another lesson here: What happens when you can't physically stop for every single hurting person you see? What happens when you can't afford to cover the bills for everyone who needs financial help? What happens when the help and love the whole world needs is far outside our abilities?

There is good news. This is not a story about bad guys and good guys. It's a story about a *specific* guy.

Jesus.

Jesus is the good Samaritan in the story.

We want to be like him, 100 percent. That's the goal. We want to "go and do likewise" and love every single fellow human. But don't miss this: the intent of Jesus telling this story was to make the point that we can't earn salvation through works. We can't find our identity through what we do. We can't rely on our own power. None of us can bandage up every hurting person we see in front of us, on TV, and online, and afford to pay for every single person's full medical bills until the day we die. If salvation was all based on works, none of us would make the cut.

We must put our faith in Jesus as the Savior. We must rely on His power. That's how we are saved. And that's how anyone can be saved. He's the only way people are getting healed from hurt, heartbreak, and sin. We are not the ultimate solution. Jesus is.

But Jesus said, "Go and do likewise." So what now? If we *can't* do everything the good Samaritan did for every single person alive, what *can* we do?

Saint Augustine of Hippo, an esteemed fourth-century theologian and bishop who influenced the development of Western Christianity, suggested that we are the innkeepers in the story. Jesus brings people to us and tells us that whatever we need, He will provide. We are to be wise with His resources, the money He's blessed us with, and the talents He has given us, and use it all so we can serve, love, and partner with Him to restore the people He's placed right in front of us.[2] I love that. I'm convicted by that.

What if you and I took on this perspective?

- While at our inns, at our posts, in our homes, at our jobs, in our classrooms—are we using all we have been given to care for those Jesus has brought into our lives?
- At our churches—are we faithfully giving and serving?
- With our own families—are we being available and forgiving?
- To our coworkers—are we being inviting and encouraging?
- Are we using our time, our resources, and the things we are good at in order to love and serve those right beside us, right here, right now?

You and I might be tempted to be the ultimate rescuer in someone's story. But Jesus is the One with all the compassion and all of the resources. Jesus can heal things we can't. Jesus can redeem things we can't. Jesus is the hero of the story.

> Jesus is the hero of the story.

Where do we go from here?

If we can't save the world, then what's our role? Are we not called to go into the world and tell the story of Jesus?

Absolutely. All of us are. That's what you will find in this book.

My prayer is that, as you read, you will discover how you actually can, in today's world, where you are, with what you have, show Jesus to those right next to you.

It's going to be fun. That's where we'll go. But that's not where we'll begin.

THE POWER WE NEED

Jesus came to this world (serving), lived in this world (showing us how to serve), and after He died and rose again, before He ascended from this world, He said, *"Here's the knowledge you need:* you will receive power when the Holy Spirit comes on you. And you will be My witnesses, first here in Jerusalem, then beyond to Judea and Samaria, and finally to the farthest places on earth" (Acts 1:8).

For years I read this verse and mistakenly put the emphasis on the end of the verse, stacking insurmountable weight on my shoulders that I must physically *go* to places on earth far from where I am in order to effectively show God's love to anyone. Perhaps you have too. Some of us *are* called to go to places far from where we are. Certainly, if that's you, *do it*. I'm rooting you on. But that's not the sole point of Jesus' commission. It's also not the order. I used to get this so very wrong. The truth is that before we go, we must first receive His power. In order, here's what Jesus was saying:

1. **We are filled with the power of the Holy Spirit.** We cannot miss this first step. Those of us who have received Jesus into our lives have that same power that raised Him from the dead living inside of us (Rom. 8:10–11). *I know, right?* It's amazing. Many of us want to go into the world, but we skip being filled with His power. We want to go with our own strategies, our own preferences, and our own handpicked people and plans. That is often our first mistake. It is when we are filled with our own power and motives that we push people away, grow frustrated, and end up depleted. We want God's power, God's strength, God's wisdom, not ours.

2. **We find our identity in Jesus.** We're *His* messengers. We're neither alone nor anonymous. We belong to Christ. We are identified with Him. We discover more of who we are when we sit in His presence, read His Word, love His Word, know Him, and talk to Him every day of our lives. Jesus' commission is not solely task-oriented, as many have come to interpret it. It's an invitation to be known and to belong.

3. **Filled and found, we go forth.** Once we are identified with Him and fueled by His power, we pass on the hope we've seen, relay the love we've experienced, and are the vocal eyewitness accounts of what Jesus Christ can do in people's lives. In order of this scripture, we are filled and found, then we go forth to

the people right next to us,[a] then to people a little farther, then to people not like us,[b] and then together our mission is to share the story of Jesus to everybody, everywhere.

Before we continue on this journey together, we must begin by being filled with His power and found in Him. Our big brother in the faith, Paul, reminded us that we can "no longer rely on ourselves and that we must trust solely in God, who possesses the power to raise the dead" (2 Cor. 1:9).

I want everyone to know Jesus for real. I want the people in my life to know how loved they are. I want to represent God's love well on social media, at Thanksgiving dinner with my family, and in line at Trader Joe's. But now I know: Relying on my own power? That's how (not) to save the world. I need the power of God. And so do you. Before we go forth, let's first be found and filled. Let's come to God in an honest prayer.

Have you lived a life of striving? A life of guilt? Have you found your identity in the outcome of what you do?

Have you grown apathetic? Have you given up on your loved ones

---

a. Jesus' listeners were standing on Jerusalem soil. People around them shared in their culture and likely their heritage and views of life. This was their starting point. This is also ours. Filled with the Spirit, and belonging to Jesus, tell His story and show what He is like to the people closest to you, in your home, in your college dorm room, in your synchronized swimming class.

b. Judea was the greater area surrounding Jerusalem, and Samaria was the region next door. People in Judea would have had cultural similarities to the Jews hearing Jesus' words, even if they were geographically farther away. Samaria, which was physically closer to Jerusalem than the outskirts of Judea, had a far different culture. Samaritans had a completely different worldview. They had different hurts, different challenges, and different perspectives. This example should remind us that some of the people closest to us in proximity see the world profoundly differently and often these relationships will take more listening, intentionality, and consistency for us to understand their lens and effectively show them how loved they are.

far from God? Have you decided that your involvement in God's mission is not important?

I invite you to join me in surrendering the shame, the fears, and the pride that have held us back from living the lives He has called us to live. Your prayer could go something like this:

> God, help me to see how I can partner with You on Your mission.
> I surrender my guilt, my pride, and any lie from the Enemy I've
> believed that has held me back from living as You've called me to
> live. I want to know the truth. As I read through the pages of this
> book, help me see the ways I can actually reveal Your love to the
> people right next to me. I want to be filled with Your power, and
> found in Your presence. And from that place, show me how I can
> go forth, amen.

Imagine a world where we all pray a prayer like this, where every Jesus-follower goes forth filled and fueled by God's power before anything else.

WHERE WE COME IN

It has been more than two decades since I sat frozen and fearful, watching lives stolen on the street right in front of me. With each following occurrence of violence, murder, and hate I have seen, my heart's sadness for the brokenness of the world has rapidly increased. There are days I still wrestle with relying on my own power. There have been times I have puffed up my chest, determined to be a long-awaited solution. There have been other times I've been so overwhelmed I let my mind spiral in thoughts of defeat. I wish I could somehow go back in time and tell that nine-year-old girl debilitated with guilt, "You are not supposed to be the one to save everyone. Anytime you feel this way, for the rest of your life, I want you to remember: There is a Savior for this world. But you're not it."

You and I cannot save the world.

But make no mistake, Jesus' mission for the saving of souls will absolutely require our participation. At our inn, among our peers, in our city, and throughout every nation, people will need to find out about the One who saves lives. We'll have to tell the people we love about Him. We have to show His kindness and compassion to them so they will know what He's like. People have to know about the freeing, hope-filled life that's available to them in order to believe. They'll have to believe to be saved (Rom 10:14–15).

First, they have to know. And that's where we come in.

How (not) to Save the World

#2 | Go Big or Get Out

Mrs. Lee opened the door.

A young man with a vacuum cleaner offered to give her a demonstration in hopes of selling the state-of-the-art cleaning device. This was long before Amazon Prime and YouTube tutorials; rest assured, door-to-door salesmen were the original Instagram influencers. She didn't need a vacuum but invited him in anyway and offered him a glass of ice-cold water, greatly appreciated on this salesman's long, soliciting Saturday. They sat across an off-white, worn-out oval wooden table with countless scratches scattered across the surface, a coral plastic bag underneath one of its legs to even out its height, and a leaf in the middle, the kind that makes tables bigger when you need to seat more people or play an aggressive card game. Concluding casual chitchat, she asked him about his life. Where was he from? What did he do to fill up his days? After beats of silence accompanied by obnoxious tap-water slurping, he reluctantly began to share.

He had just entered a recovery program after years of heroin addiction. He told her about his days in a gang and showed bullet-wound scars in his calves from running from the police after multiple robberies. He spoke of the women he mistreated, the men he owed money to, and the people he was still running away from. He revealed he had been in a never-ending cycle for years—trying to get clean but going back to his old ways over and over again. Head hung low, he confessed he wasn't sure where his life was headed or if he could ever turn his life completely around.

Mrs. Lee showed no shock and spoke no shame. Instead, she shared her story of searching and stumbling as well, her years of being unsure of who she was and what she was living for. Story after story, these two strangers learned they had more in common than anyone could have predicted. The details that filled their lives were vastly different, and yet they were bonded by a void they both spent years trying to fill. Then Mrs. Lee told him about a man named Jesus—a man who had healed the broken pieces of her shattered heart and paid the penalty for everything she had ever done. She told him how her life had never been this whole, peaceful, or joy-filled and that this same Jesus was available for him too. She spoke of how Jesus came to the world to make it possible for him to come to God without any guilt or shame. She told him how much God loved him and about a brand-new life available to him, if he wanted it.

Leaning in across that old, uneven table, she asked, "Do you want to change your life?"

He did.

Right then and there, on his knees, in the middle of a stranger's cold, faded black-and-white-checkered floor, that young salesman gave his life to Jesus . . . and he would never be the same.

Mrs. Lee didn't know that five years later that man would begin an outreach to those living on the streets of San Francisco, pastoring and discipling those with a past in prison and addiction like himself for the rest of his life. She certainly didn't know that more than three decades later, I'd be at my own kitchen table, typing about how she led my dad to Christ. She passed away without ever knowing the lives that would be changed because of that one opened door and one conversation across the old, uneven wooden table. But I will never forget.

YOUR TURN

I was eleven years old, sitting across from my dad, playing one of our favorite games, Guess Who? It was an ordinary day—I had just watched him lead more than two dozen people on the streets to Jesus, and now we were hurrying to get one more board game in before dinnertime. As I pulled a card from the game's raddled cardboard box, I asked him, "Dad, who led *you* to Jesus?" Wide-eyed, with my feet drumming against the floor, I expected a story at least as striking as the ones I had witnessed in our beloved city park. An out-of-body, cosmic experience, perhaps a famous preacher calling him out from the stage at a conference he once attended, or at least something involving fireworks, thunder, or glitter (those were the days of Lisa Frank stickers and Mariah Carey posters plastered across young girls' rooms, so, you know, glitter was big).

Nonchalantly chuckling, my dad responded, "A woman I tried to sell a vacuum to." He looked up from our board game. "Your turn."

My feet were now at a standstill. "Wait, what?" Refusing to continue playing without a satisfying answer, I leaned toward him, waiting for clarification, forcing his gaze to meet mine. "That's not very exciting. I want the *whole* story."

As he shared this very unspectacular account of him coming to Jesus at a kitchen in the Twin Peaks district of the city, a story he admitted he never thought about anymore, my disappointment faded. My posture perked up. My curiosity grew. I had so many more questions. "Did you ever see her again? Does she know what happened to you after? Why have you never told us this story?"

He laughed, simply wanting to keep playing our game, the smells of stir-fry summoning from the kitchen like a timer signaling us to speed up. "Hosanna, that's all that happened. Go, it's your turn."

Throughout the week I replayed that story in my bustling middle-school mind and something inside of me began to awaken.

Up until that point, I had always believed that I had to do something big in order to do something important. My dad was a truth-telling preacher, my mom was a compassionate teacher and championship-winning volleyball coach, and my older sister was a powerhouse singer and songwriter, singing and leading at churches and events. I had none of those skills. My younger brother was only five at the time, so I did have a bit of pride that I was at least smarter and taller than somebody in the family.[a]

I never thought of my life as all that significant, nor did I imagine that it ever would be. I figured I would support whatever the rest of my family was doing. I wasn't necessarily torn up about that; I loved my family and was amazed by all the remarkable things they did. I just knew I was the supporting cast. I wasn't special. I wasn't obviously skilled. I wasn't popular. I was just Hosanna. Important people did spectacular things, and I was profoundly ordinary.

Then I heard about Mrs. Lee.

---

a. By the way, that didn't last long. My brother is by far the smartest out of all of us, and he is six foot one while I'm a mighty five foot four—okay, technically five foot three-and-a-half inches. My growth spurt is still coming, in the name of Jesus.

This woman didn't preach to hundreds of people every week. She didn't run organizations or lead movements. Yet right where she was, during her normal routine, as she went about her ordinary life, she saw an opportunity to get to know someone and speak truth to someone who may have needed some hope—and she did. She simply paid attention to a need right in front of her. Precisely where she already was. She opened her door. What if she hadn't? What would my dad's life have looked like? What would *my* life have looked like?

Mrs. Lee was a woman not insecure about the lack of luster in her humble home. She was a woman not distracted by the results of her decisions. Unfazed by the lack of an audience or the possible embarrassment of rejection, she did not know the effects of her everyday choices, and she didn't need to.

She knew something it took me years to learn. Thinking I have to go big or get out? That's how (not) to save the world. That lie stops us from loving those right next to us. The truth is better. We don't have to do something impressive to do something important.

When we define our significance by the splendor of our skills or our purpose by the applause for our actions, we miss out on specific, pivotal ways God wants to use exactly who we are, where we are, to open the door for those right in front of us. And that helps a grand total of no one. Some of the clearest calls God has given us are being ignored because we're measuring their impact by our own egotistical standards, proving we are more concerned with the sensationalism of spirituality than the literal saving of souls.

> God wants to use exactly who we are, where we are, to open the door for those right in front of us.

Lots of Jesus-followers want a story like Mrs. Lee's. We want to notice people who knock on our door. We want to be compassionate question-askers, with ears ready to listen. We want to offer people a new and better life and never complicate God's call. We want our lives to be meaningful and effective.

But there's a problem.

Most of us don't believe we can do it right, say it right, or close the deal. We don't think we have the right amount of spiritual skills, have the correct level of schooling, or know the exact theology to introduce someone to Jesus as best as He deserves. Our fear of dropping the ball and ruining the introduction to Jesus causes us to never say anything, invite people to anything, or talk about Christ in our lives at all. *If this isn't going to have a big impact on someone's life, why even try? If I'm just going to embarrass myself, who does that help? It'd be safer to say nothing. After all, I don't fully understand the mission. I'm not the right person. This is not the right time.* We step back, believing every single one of these lies.

The truth might shock us.

God does not just have the ability to use ordinary people, He also has the desire. We are His first choice. As God calls us, He's not calling in the bench, the B team, or the practice squad. He's calling in His starters. We are His plan A. The Creator of the universe, with endless power and resources, has handmade His best plan for humans to know how much He loves them.

It's you. It's me.

Put me in, Coach.

God does extraordinary things through those who are ordinary. (And those who are just plain extra! Can I get an amen?) Regardless of your title, socioeconomic status, family background, regardless of whether you are married or not, highly educated or not, impressive to others or not, you are *exactly* who God wants to open the door in front of you. Don't wait for someone else. You are who He wants to use. And

He wants to use you now. Not next week, not after you get a degree, not after you are married with two-and-a-half kids. But at your inn, at your door, at your table, today.

HATERS GONNA HATE

If you have ever felt like you are not living up to other people's expectations, you are in good company. Jesus did not live a life that was up to the aristocratic standards of His culture either. Many religious people of His day were waiting for a leader who would be an enforcer of religion, a conqueror of other religions, and the catalyst to a greater movement of more religious people. But Jesus coming to earth actually had nothing to do with religion. He came because we were broken, and we had no other way to be healed and whole and to come back to God. He came to be the solution.

Many disapproved of His methods. In fact, Jesus had a track record of letting lots of religious people down. (Perhaps you can relate. I know I can.)

In Luke 19 we meet a man named Zacchaeus, a dishonest and deceitful tax collector, a sellout and a snitch, who cheated people and stole money for personal gain.[b] Jesus was passing through the

---

b. *The role of tax collectors.* Tax collectors were private government subcontractors who "earned a profit by demanding a higher tax from the people than they had prepaid to the Roman government. This system led to widespread greed and corruption. The tax-collecting profession was saturated with unscrupulous people who overtaxed others to maximize their personal gain. . . . Since the Jews considered themselves victims of Roman oppression, Jewish tax collectors who overtaxed their fellow countrymen were especially despised." Jeffrey E. Miller, "Tax Collector," in *The Lexham Bible Dictionary* (Bellingham, WA: Lexham Press, 2016).

The Roman government preferred hiring locals who knew the lay of the land best. This caused another level of personal grief to those being taxed. Imagine your own cousin

town, Zacchaeus climbed up a tree for a good view, and Jesus invited him down. "Zacchaeus, hurry down from that tree," signaled Jesus, "because I need to stay at your house *tonight*" (Luke 19:5). The crowd was not impressed. They grumbled at the notion He would stay and eat with this man, saying, "He has gone to be the guest of a notorious sinner" (Luke 19:7 NLT).

Jesus beckoned Matthew, also a despised tax collector, and said, "Follow me." Then "as Jesus sat down to eat in Matthew's house, many tax collectors and sinners joined Jesus and his disciples at the table" (Matt. 9:9–10 CEB). Jesus was having all these dinner parties, and the Pharisees were livid. *This is not how it's done,* they surely thought. *Doesn't this "Savior" know how to be a religious leader? Doesn't He know who to eat with and who to avoid?* In their minds, Jesus was doing it the wrong way, saying the wrong things, and spending time, *wasting* time, with the wrong people.

Jesus was repeatedly giving invitations and having conversations with people He came across. He was opening doors and sitting at tables.

> Jesus was known for the relationships He had. He wants us to be too.

When any one of us consistently accepts invitations and frequents conversations with someone, we form an ongoing relationship. You likely don't have a relationship with anyone you've never given an invitation to, received an invitation from, or had a conversation with.

Jesus loved spending time with everyday people so much that even Jesus' haters defined Him by His relationships. The religious people

---

being a subcontractor. Your own neighbor being a locally hired tax collector. And these people close to you taking an additional tax for themselves over the tax they needed to truly charge you. This was more than robbery. It was betrayal by an acquaintance, friend, or family member. Who would love those people?

scolded Him, reprimanding Him as "a friend of tax collectors and sinners" (Luke 7:34 NIV). They thought this was one of the greatest accusations imaginable. *Ha! We got Him! Friend of sinners! Good one!* But for Jesus, this name was a sign of success because it was the very definition of His mission. Jesus came to be with people, to invite people to follow Him, and to continuously talk about things with them. He'd listen to them and they'd listen to Him; they'd have interesting, ongoing conversations and form invested, ongoing relationships. Jesus was known for the relationships He had. He wants us to be too. That may not be up to the bougie^c standards we have for what we think Christians should look like, speak like, and live like. Just like the religious people of Jesus' day, our standards may be wrong.

EVERYBODY LOVES GOOD FOOD

What can *we* do if our everyday lives feel underwhelming, our skills aren't obvious, and our platforms aren't booming? We can open doors and sit at tables. We can freely welcome, pursue, and form genuine relationships without living in debilitating fear of the end results. We can find common ground through our imperfect stories and shared interests. We can let people know that they are seen and what they are going through is important to us.

You may be thinking, *friendships don't lead people to Jesus.* We can't just have a bunch of friends. We need to share the gospel, the good news of Jesus! That's fair. We will get there. But we must start

---

c. *Bougie* is a slang term that means "Oh, you fancy!" Or, more likely, you want to come off as fancy. It's said to come from the term *bourgeois*, meaning the middle class trying to come off as rich or as materialistic as the upper class. (I like my definition better. Both work. Try it out. Making it mean whatever you want would certainly be a bougie thing to do.)

here. Why would anyone believe that the God we serve wants to know them if we don't even want to know them? How do we share about Jesus, Immanuel, "God with us," who came to be with them, when we don't even spend time with them? If we are not careful, we will self-righteously aim to save the world and skip knowing the world we claim we want to reach.

What Is the Good News?

The story of Jesus is often called the good news—not a good idea, not a good theory. It's an announcement about something that actually happened. It's a report on an event that occurred.

The first eyewitnesses of Jesus who went from city to city to tell His story were relaying an event that they saw, that happened, that changed them, and they were passing the truth on. The headlines had been bleak: The World Is Broken. People Are Hopeless. We Are Headed Toward Death. Jesus' first disciples experienced something completely different and went to proclaim new headlines. We Can Be Healed. We Can Have Hope. We Can Have Life for Forever. Jesus Happened. Jesus Has Made a Way. There is better news than we've ever imagined. There is a greater report than we ever knew was possible. And thousands of years later, we are called to share this same good news.

This is why I share it: Jesus happened for me.

An event occurred. I was broken, hopeless, and divided from God, and then I gave Jesus my whole life, and now I'm on a journey toward wholeness, freedom, and joy like I've never known. I'm not the same. And I want to tell you about it. I now know I am loved and have purpose. And I want you to know what's available to you too. *Jesus died for us and rose again, and now we can leave behind our old lives and have a brand-new, hope-filled life in Him.*

We get the word gospel from the Greek word for "good news." When we say we are sharing the gospel, we are announcing something extraordinary. A headline that changes lives. The true story of how Jesus came to save the world, brought it hope and healing, and is now available for every single one of us. Jesus happened. Jesus is still happening. Jesus heals. And His healing is still happening. This news is good. I hope everybody hears it.

So who can you open a door for? What table can you sit at?

Going to all of your friends' kids' soccer games and out to pizza with them afterward may not result in all of them coming to church with you on Sunday. That is no reason to not start selfless relationships with the people God has put in your life. Muddy fields, melted-ice-filled coolers, and squeezed-out Capri Suns may not seem as picturesque as people getting on their knees and worshipping God in arenas. But your friends aren't in those arenas. They are at their kids' scrimmage games. Who knows what doors your friendships open? Who knows the lifelong impact you could be leaving by simply showing up for people and letting them feel loved and supported? Don't let ordinary stop you from being obedient.

Saying yes to an invitation from your neighbors to go over to their house for dinner may seem quaint and even inconvenient. You know they aren't interested in anything related to religion, and you feel you could never lead them to Jesus. Don't let results stand in the way of having relationships. Jesus sat at many tables with people where there's no record if they ultimately followed Him. The

> Don't let ordinary stop you from being obedient.

religious people of His day did not see the point of that. They wanted Jesus to guilt, shame, and punish people, and Jesus wanted to forgive them, accept them, and enjoy their company. Jesus was motivated by His love for people. He was interested in people. He left His position with God to come to earth *for* people. To be *with* people. Filled with exuberant life and unconditional love for people, the Savior of the world spent a lot of His life enjoying good food, laughing loudly, attending weddings, telling stories, and creating memories alongside friends.

There is no training course we must graduate from in order to have lively relationships with those around us. There is no certificate we must have on our wall before we can serve those in need in our workplaces. We do not need to be biblical scholars in order to do real life with real people, ask honest questions, and give honest answers. As we give invitations and have conversations, cultivating commonality with those around us, we begin to know people—people God really loves. And people begin to know us. Like any ongoing friendship, as you are continuously honest and open, over time the most important things in your life naturally seep out in your conversations and through your actions. They will naturally discover who Jesus is to you, learning that He is a big deal in their friend's life, the reason their friend is joyful, kind, purpose-filled, and resilient. When you don't know where to start, remember: Everybody loves good food. And everybody loves good friends.

FILL THE GAP

Mrs. Lee didn't second-guess if she was the right person at that exact moment when she met my dad. To her, the mission was clear. The person was her. The time was now. This young man didn't know Jesus, and he was at *her* door. She knew what Jesus could do for him, and based on her own experience, she knew how God could transform his life. She didn't complicate God's call. To her, the choice to share Jesus was simple. Whether or not he accepted Him wasn't up to her.

Her story changed everything for me when I was a little girl. No longer would I compare myself to my older sister, who sang in ways I never could, or to my dad, who preached in ways I never would. Instead, I simply became more aware and available for whatever needs might arise. At our outreach with our friends on the streets, I became the chief gap-filler. I figured if I couldn't do anything else, I could at least focus on finding things that needed to be done. More and more I began noticing the chairs that needed to be cleaned, the clothes that needed to be folded, the lunches that were not yet packed. I started hanging out with more kids on the streets, no longer putting on the pressure for us to be lifelong friends afterward, and no longer being in a hurry when someone asked me to stop and pray for them. I felt a new sense of purpose in my every move. If Jesus was simply all about people, then I would be too.

How would our lives be different if we stopped seeing the call to share Jesus as a rigid mandate to convert and instead saw it as the freedom to continuously make invitations and have conversations with those right next to us? How would our days be spent differently if we knew the mission of Jesus was not a call to make people more religious but a call to have more relationships?

I believe we would stop comparing ourselves to others. We would stop living in fear of what others think about us. We would stop making excuses for why we're not the *right* people for God to use for *this* particular task or *this* exact person at *this* specific time. We would start to engage more with our neighbors. We would go the extra mile for a coworker's birthday, giving them a card with encouraging words about what we enjoy about them and how we're thankful for them and adding in a ten-dollar gift card. (Who doesn't feel loved by a few extra dollars to go to Starbucks? Zero people. It's science.[d]) We would find ways to say, "Yes, I'll be there!" when our friends invite us to their band's upcoming gig, letting them know we're interested in their lives instead of repeatedly defaulting to "maybe some other time." We would take more risks. We would not live from a place of exhaustion but a place of excitement, eager to show the love of Jesus whenever and however we can. We would realize that every day is an opportunity to open up that door a little more.

If that happened, I believe—I *know*—the world would look a lot different.

More people would feel seen. More people would know they are loved. More people would know what it's like when someone is *for* them and *with* them.

God's mission would be carried out.[e]

I once thought I had to do something big to make an impact for God. I thought I had to go big or get out. That lie has stopped me from reaching out and getting to know the people around me. Perhaps that lie has stopped you too. God has a better way. Make invitations and have conversations right where you are. Be aware, and be available. Be a gap-filler, and be a good friend. Love the people right next to you as if God's love is revealed through your everyday life. Because it is.

The mission is clear. The people are us. The time is now. Every day

---

d. It's not science. Just to make sure my publisher doesn't get in trouble: not actual science. (But sort of science.)

e. Our mission is an overflow of God's ultimate mission. God wants to be with us. He wants to have a restored relationship with every person alive. Our mission is to partner with Him in accomplishing His mission. The mission is not ours alone. It's His. And since He cares about it more than we do, He designed us and equipped us for this very purpose.

of our lives is an opportunity to make someone feel seen, known, and loved. When we
put results over relationships, we're doing it
wrong. When we see people as projects, we're
doing it wrong. We are not called to save the
world. We are called to open doors and sit

**The mission is clear.
The people are us.
The time is now.**

at tables. We are called to start and continue authentic relationships.
Once we do, we'll start having better meals, sharing better stories, and
needing bigger tables.

YOU DON'T HAVE TO DO SOMETHING *Big* IN ORDER TO DO SOMETHING *Important*

How (not) to Save the World

#3 | Check the Easy Box

When I was eighteen years old, my dad died from cancer. My little brother, Elijah, was twelve.

Elijah shut down emotionally and would not speak to my mom, our older sister, Candace, or me about what he was feeling. It seemed there was no way to connect with him. It did not help that when someone would see us at church, they'd pray over us, saying things like "God is going to use this for your testimony one day,"[a] and turn to leave. Or say, "God's going to take care of you," but not ask what physical needs we may have had in that moment.

---

a. At its core definition, a testimony is a recounting and retelling of a personal experience. You give your testimony in a court of law about what you went through, what you know, or what you have seen. When Christ-followers use the term in the context of sharing about Jesus, it typically means the recounting and retelling of our personal experiences with Jesus, the stories of what we went through, what we know of Him, and what we have seen. Though we can tend to overspiritualize the concept of "sharing my testimony" and at times use it to talk more about us than to talk about God, at its core it's the true story of what we have experienced. At its best, it reveals the real power of God and how He redeems real lives.

I'll never forget running into one of our church's most popular and spiritual women at our neighborhood's corner market. She stopped Elijah and me and said, "Don't worry, kids; you know your daddy is swimming in the crystal waters and running down the streets of gold! Don't be sad; he's not sad! He's in a better place," then she continued shopping.

I remember standing there with my brother and saying, "There's no way Dad is swimming."

"Totally," he replied.

For a long period of time it felt like people were saying things *at* us. *God is going to use this for good. God has a plan. Your dad is in a better place.* But *we* were not in a good place.

Many people seemed to be very concerned if we had the correct, official theology about the holy transition of our family's patriarch from one side of eternity to the next. They seemed less concerned that we suddenly lost the best person we ever knew, who knew how to comfort us as well as how to cook incredible chow mein and *nuòmǐ fàn*[b] for dinner, who laughed at all our jokes and made up silly songs for just about anything. (One of our favorites was his song about my mom, "I Met Her on the Basketball Court," about how, after she fouled him, he knew she was the one. There's something both endearing and disturbing about that. We don't have time to unpack all of it here.) It didn't feel like we were allowed to be sad or angry or not yet writing out our testimony to lead many to Jesus through this tragic loss.

My brother took this the hardest. All of a sudden, there was no man in his life. Just a lot of speeches about how the man who *was* in

---

b. *Nuòmǐ fàn*, or sticky rice, is a life-changing Chinese rice dish. My family and I will typically add shiitake mushrooms, Chinese sausage, and green onions. Sometimes bamboo shoots and shrimp too. Top it off with some cilantro and oyster sauce, and you'll be filled with the Holy Spirit. (Or at least, you'll be *filled*!) If you ever come over to my house, I'll make some for you.

his life was now in a better place than being on earth with him. It is no wonder my brother shut down.

At eighteen I learned how *not* to speak to people who were hurting and grieving. It didn't take long for me to realize that up until that point, I, too, had been insensitive to my friends in their losses. I had performed profound monologues at my friend whose boyfriend broke up with her, without asking her what I could do and what fun activity we could venture off to in order to get her mind off that horrid breaker of hearts. I had not listened to Taylor Swift songs on the floor beside her, swiftly empowering her with the message that she was too good for him anyway and you *are never getting back together, like, ever.*[1] I had prayed over people who were stressed out about finances, telling them that God would provide, without asking what kind of job they were looking for, asking people in my community if they had any odd jobs available, and then following up with them later to see if there were any other needs. I had heard the best sermons growing up and was practically an expert at reciting message bullet points to people who were in need. But I had not been good at listening to their needs, weeping with them while their hearts hurt, and intentionally immersing myself in what they were going through.

My friends heard me declare the important morals I held and the sacred traditions I followed, as if Jesus was all about following rules. And yet I failed at making those around me feel seen, known, and loved, as if Jesus was all about loving people.

It's easy for us to check the easy box. Say the correct theological thing about heaven to this twelve-year-old boy who lost his dad. Pray the most eloquent prayer at church against racism in our world. Post the best graphics with the coolest colors that speak against human trafficking. All the while not considering what sort of activities you could invite that young boy to, not rethinking the systemic racial biases in your own company and implementing new policies to eradicate such biases, or not pledging to give monthly toward an anti-trafficking organization's safe-house initiatives. Those alternative choices would take a great deal of time and investment. They'd take energy. They'd take commitment. *To continuously support this ministry? To constantly reconsider the prejudice in my company? To commit to having this boy over to our family's house once a month and becoming a mentor to him? Gosh.* Our lives are actually very busy. And though our hearts are in the right place, most of us would prefer a way to help those hurting people that didn't require so much time and energy.

BADGERS AND AMBASSADORS

I did not know how to speak to my brother. I didn't handle his hurt perfectly. Thankfully I didn't give him strange religious speeches, but I didn't have anything better to say either. I was away at college, hundreds of miles away, and I would call and ask how he was doing, but all he wanted to do was talk about comic books. I couldn't get any emotion out of him, not even grief. He would merely respond to my questions with the new cool things he discovered in the latest Marvel or DC comic he was reading. (Did you know the Hulk was originally supposed to be gray, not green? And Wolverine was nearly named the Badger? You're welcome. Love, Elijah.)

If I wanted to have a relationship with my brother, I had to start reading comic books. I had always loved superheroes, but mostly with a shallow, what-I've-seen-on-TV level of love. *This* was going to take some deep diving into secondhand comic bookstores and getting lost in the layers of cosmic universes and the psyches of mad scientists.

So that's what I did. I fell in love with what he loved. I learned how he saw the world. Over the next couple months, whenever I'd call him, we'd have a lot to talk about. When I visited, we'd go to thrift stores and try to find hidden treasures. We had never been closer. I started to see the world as he saw it, not how I saw it. And this world had way cooler monsters, planets, and explosions.

When we take the time to learn someone's lens of the world, we can speak more effectively into their real life. So often we want to do the *right* thing, say the *right* thing, but we don't consider the context of who is listening on the other end of our perfected speeches. We get to pat ourselves on the back that we reached out to someone or we said the spiritual one-liner we've been trained to say, all the while not truly helping anyone.

> When we take the time to learn someone's lens of the world, we can speak more effectively into their real life.

I had to learn this the hard way. Checking the easy box? That's how (not) to save the world.

To be Christ's ambassadors (2 Cor. 5:20), we will need to know two things:

1. **The words and ways of those around us.** In essence, we need to know people's personal languages. This does not solely mean the dialect of someone from another country or culture. This also means the worldview, the cultural lens, and the current feelings of someone who technically speaks the same language as you. What has your teammate gone through this year? What past hurts from the church do your neighbors have? What has your coworker been struggling with? What is your little brother's favorite comic book character? Have you spent the time with these people to ask these questions? Their unique answers

will change how you speak specifically to each and every one of them. For some of us, we know the words of God, but we are not sure of the languages or lenses of the people in our lives.

2. **The words and ways of God.** For some of us, we know the language of the world around us, but we are unprepared to speak on behalf of God. To be effective messengers, we need to consistently be reading the Word of God so we know what He is like, what He says, and how He speaks. Peter urged us to "always be prepared to give an answer to everyone who asks you to give the reason for the hope that you have. But do this with gentleness and respect" (1 Pet. 3:15 NIV). We need to be knee-deep in the words of Jesus and the ways of God, our Father, so that we are already prepared to speak with truthfulness, gentleness, and respect whenever a door opens.

We can easily read Peter's words about being prepared to give answers and say, "Okay! Just tell me what words to prepare! What's the speech?" But again, this won't be a memorized speech that can be copied and pasted to every single person alive without knowing anything about them. That's checking the easy box. That's the solution many of us prefer. *Isn't there some solution to brokenness that doesn't take so much time? Is there a way for souls to be saved that doesn't take so much energy?* What Jesus calls us to is a life of intentionally listening to Him, listening to others, opening doors, sitting at tables, having relationships, and speaking to people in ways they understand. A memorized speech won't be in everyone's language, relevant to everyone's lens, and able to answer their specific heart's most burning questions. Some of us know scriptures by heart, can quote a mini sermon at any point, and can give the theological reasoning behind many of our church's most sacred teachings, but we don't know the questions people around us are actually asking, the hurts they are feeling, or the needs they have.

We must be good listeners of people and good learners of the Word of God. In a sense, we must become bilingual, learning both languages and lenses to communicate as clearly and effectively as possible. We need to know the questions people are asking and know God's answers to their questions.

This won't happen by accident. This will take reading the Word of God with more frequency and intentionality. This will take reaching out to your friends to ask how they are, asking your teammates about their lives, showing up to your neighbor's sports games, going to your friends' school plays, creating dinner parties at your home, and offering to spend time with and speak life to someone younger than you.

This will not be checking the easy box, but this will be what it takes to speak effectively into people's lives. It may ruin your routines, push your plans, and take up more time than you anticipated. It may look like reaching out to those who don't reach out to you and caring for those who don't yet care for you. It may look like forgiving those who hurt you or canceling anticipated plans to mourn with someone who lost a loved one. This is the tough stuff. This calling is not cute. This will be the hard, humbling work, the dying-to-yourself work, getting your favorite clothes drenched in fresh mud to be in the dirt with people who are feeling defeated on an active battlefield. As we enter the sacred spaces of people's hurting hearts, we will need to leave our egos on the sidelines. But we're talking about resurrection. Actual resurrection. If we want to see people once dead in sin raised

> If we want to see people once dead in sin raised to life in Jesus, healed, and restored by His power, we might have to be uncomfortable sometimes.

to life in Jesus, healed, and restored by His power, we might have to be uncomfortable sometimes.

DEAFENING

Both my parents were deaf in one ear. They could hear each other best when my dad was on the left of my mom, as if he were the driver in an American car, ensuring that family conversations were livelier and funnier whenever we were out driving somewhere. Growing up, we kids frequently made the mistake of shouting louder in a grocery store to find them or screaming more intensely into their deaf ears for them to hear us, but that didn't help and would typically give them headaches. The best way for us to be heard was not to shout across the room or to be louder where no sound could possibly come through, but to instead get up from where we were, walk up to them, touch their shoulder, get their attention, and speak toward their good ear.

Getting louder isn't always the best way to be heard.

Getting closer to where people are is better.

When I lived in Beijing, China, for a few months, I knew I had to learn as much of the language as I could. I had picked up very little Cantonese from my dad, plus the people in the area I was in mostly spoke Mandarin, and my family's dialect would not suffice to demonstrate to my neighbors how much I respected them or my desire to communicate with them.

> Getting louder isn't always the best way to be heard.

Foreigners have an off-putting tendency to shout their own language louder at someone who only understands their native tongue. Though *we* are the outsiders in *their* land, we tend to speak our own language at locals instead of putting in the effort to learn their tongue, and when they don't understand, we can get frustrated, defensive, and pompously proclaim louder, "Where is the nearest restaurant? You don't understand me? *Where is the nearest restaurant?*"

Even louder, they still don't speak your language. Volume is not the ultimate translator. Yelling doesn't make them feel respected or like they can ever have a conversation with you. And you will go hungry not knowing where the nearest restaurant is. What a bummer that would be. (Not as significant of a loss, of course, but almost.)

At our worst, Christians do this too. When we don't take the time to get closer to where other people are and learn how to best communicate to those around us, we can get irritated, and we hope our increased volume makes the difference. We increase our volume on social media—emphasizing arguments in all caps and doubling down on aggressive words in the comment sections with those who do not see the world like us.[c] We increase our volume in our conversations— using words that are unique to those who have read the Bible or spent time in church, terms and phrases most other people don't know: *born again, the Holy Ghost, covered by the blood, quiet time,* and many others. We speak in these superspiritual expressions to people who have never even heard the great news about Jesus, and we think that somehow checks the box of showing someone the hope found in Christ.

It doesn't. They can't understand you. No matter how loud you shout, "*The veil was torn in two and we can now be in fellowship with our heavenly Father!*" they don't know what that means. You sound crazy. And they don't want to hear anything more from you.

If we want to positively impact our world, we'll need to stop trying

---

c. It is possible to reveal God's love on social media. There is a guide in the back of this book to give us some tools. See "The Truth About Revealing God's Love Through Social Media."

to argue people to Jesus, and we'll need to drop the terms and expressions only Christians use and no one else understands. We're going to have to do the important work of learning the words and ways of the people around us, and their lens of the world, so that we can reveal the real hope found in Jesus and how that impacts their real lives.

Don't waste one day of your life checking a seemingly spiritual box that ultimately strokes your own ego, perhaps impresses other Christ-followers, but ultimately turns people away from the beauty of a real relationship with Jesus. We're not called to make ourselves known. We're called to make Jesus known. We're not called to tell people how important *we* are. We are called to tell people how loved *they* are.

> We're not called to tell people how important *we* are. We are called to tell people how loved *they* are.

The writer of 1 Corinthians 13 reminded us that we can speak the most spiritual language, do all the most publicly impressive deeds, but if we don't love people, forgive people, listen to people, exhibit patience with people, and fight for people, we're merely loud, crashing cymbals. We're screaming into ears that can't hear us. We're speaking a language others won't understand. We're causing painful, deafening, crashing cymbal-like noise online, at work, and at home. This is not how to effectively show who Jesus really is and the life He truly offers. There is a better way.

Instead of solely fighting against what's holding people back, step into their world, learn their words and ways, and fight for the relationship.

Instead of seeing people's varied hobbies and perspectives as walls, see them as doors, opportunities to invest in their interests and find commonality. Step into their world, learn their words and ways, and fight for the relationship.

Choose to fight *for* people. Listen to what hurts their hearts. Join in on the hobbies they love. Don't be angry at them for what is torn inside of them. Instead, love them as God loves all of us. "God demonstrates his own love for us in this: While we were still sinners, Christ died for us" (Rom. 5:8 NIV).

How can we demonstrate God's love to others? Before they love us, love them. Before they choose us, choose them. Before they come to us, go to them. Before they step into our world, step into theirs.

FOR LITTLE BROTHERS EVERYWHERE

I skipped my Friday classes and drove seven hours from college to walk around the San Francisco Giants stadium with Elijah during a playoff game. The ballpark sits alongside glistening San Francisco Bay flowing to the Pacific Ocean, surrounded by a bustling pier with museums, rides, restaurants, and singing seals galore. One splash zone sits beyond the right-field wall (affectionately called McCovey Cove by locals in honor of former player Willie McCovey) while tangerine- and tomato-colored kayaks fill the cove, with radical hopefuls ready to catch any splash-hits that fly into the ice-cold bay. Though we couldn't afford tickets, we could wear our Giants gear, play arcade games around the pier, and listen to the live plays on our handheld radio while hearing the thundering screams coming from the ballpark. Outside the ballpark, each of us with an ice cream cone in hand, the wind causing our napkins to fly, and the waves of the bay crashing alongside the railing in front of us, I asked Elijah, "How do you feel today?"

Elijah responded, "I'm mad."

The roaring world around us stood still. The first time he had opened up in years, I hung on to his every word. I did not have the perfect, profound words to share, so instead, I tried my best to validate his every emotion. "You're right. This is not fair. I know. This shouldn't have happened. I'm with you. I'm so mad too." Tears flowed from his face as he stared at the water, sharing about his deepest fears and most gut-wrenching regrets. I threw my arm around him, and we sat there, listening to the screeching crowds as the Giants won their playoff game, and finishing our waffle cones, with melted chocolate chip cookie dough milk pouring from the sides.

As the years continued, my brother and I continued to bond over superhero comic books and movies. As he became less interested in baseball and increasingly enamored with our home basketball team, the Golden State Warriors, I did too. We created traditions whenever I was in town, watching games at home in full-on gear or going to the newest Marvel movie and getting the biggest popcorn possible. When I married my husband, Guy, he joined our traditions.

It was about nine years after that moment on the pier when my brother told me and Guy that he wanted to give his entire life to Jesus. He was tired of being broken, angry, and half-living and wanted what we had. He knew it was Jesus. He wasn't sure how to do it perfectly or if God would accept him after all this time. He had done some things he wasn't proud of. We assured him it's never too late, no one is too far, and God is always excited for us to be closer to Him. A new, healed, and purpose-filled life was available in Jesus, if he wanted to receive it.

He did.

At first I was in shock. There had been so many times throughout the years when I wanted to give up on fighting for my brother—I was putting so much into this relationship and wasn't sure if I was doing it right or really making a difference. There were so many times I almost stopped praying for my brother. No matter how much I prayed for God to be real to him and for me to have the right words for him, it felt like my requests were falling on deaf ears, and I was starting to wonder if it was pointless. I'm so glad I never gave up. I'm so glad I never stopped praying. Friend, never stop praying for your loved ones who are far from God.[d]

As my husband and I prayed with Elijah at our kitchen table, I'm sure I didn't do it perfectly. I'm sure I didn't say all the right things and that any freshman at a Christian college could take apart the words I used one by one and explain how they weren't as theologically correct as they could have been. I'm sure many could critique how many years passed before Elijah entrusted me with this important decision. In that moment, I realized that perhaps I had put too much of an emphasis on how much all that mattered.

Elijah confessed he needed Jesus.

He told Jesus he did. He invited Jesus to be his Number One, his Savior, his Rescuer, and the Lord of his life. Guy and I prayed alongside him as he told Jesus he was turning away from a life without Him, every sin, every feeling of shame, everything separating him from God. He wanted to live for Jesus forever. We wept together, and we hugged each other. It was simple, a little strange, and yet so very sacred.

Soon my brother and I would start going through the New Testament together weekly over Zoom and discovering the person of Jesus in a new way. During our studies together we would both end up falling more in love with Jesus. But for the time being we went to get burritos at a hole-in-the-wall spot he had never been to before. He had also never had carne asada fries and was forever changed by their wonder. Everything was new.

If you want a guide of How to Perfectly Lead the Whole World to

---

d. I made a guide to help us pray for our loved ones and those far from God. See the back of the book: "A Prayer Challenge and Five-Step Guide." Let's never stop praying.

Jesus, you're reading the wrong book. I have no idea. Here's what I do know. Real people right next to you need to know they are not alone. They need to know that Jesus is with them. Why would they believe Jesus is with them if their Jesus-friends aren't with them?

- There are people in your life with real physical needs, perhaps for food, clothes, or childcare. Pray and consider how God can use you to meet those needs, and actively seek to help. Jesus cares about their physical needs, and so should we. Is there someone who needs a meal train this month? How can you organize that?
- There's someone in your community who just had their heart broken, and it would bless their life to go out to a fun dinner with friends this Valentine's Day. Jesus cares about their hurting hearts, and so should we. What's your first step in planning that?
- There's someone posting on social media about how they are struggling with loneliness. Pray for them, ask God to show you His heart for them, and thoughtfully reach out to them, asking if they need someone to talk to.

You are not called to be there for every single person in the world—that lie will bring us back to seeing ourselves as saviors and getting grossly overwhelmed. Let's just talk about one person. Let's start there. Remember that God's mission is to be with people, and to carry out His mission, He calls us to be with them too. To hear why they're hurting. To be present in their pain.

> Many times your greatest witness will be your with-ness.

Many times your greatest witness will be your with-ness.

Who will you come alongside of and be with, right where they are? Whose words and ways will you learn? Whose lens will you start to see through?

God is not asking us to stand over people but to sit with people. God is not asking us to convince people to see the world the way that we do. God is asking us to look through their lens, learn how they speak and what they like, and love them right where they are. God is asking us to really get to know people so that they can really know Him. It won't be easy, but it will change lives. It won't happen overnight, but it will defeat darkness.

For little brothers everywhere. For your coworker. For your roommate. For the barista at your favorite local coffee shop. For your neighbor across the street. Let's choose to love them first. Together, let's love our world well.

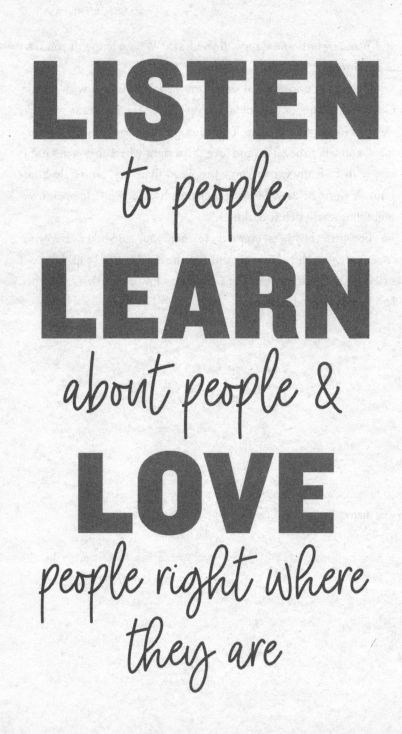

LISTEN to people **LEARN** about people & **LOVE** people right where they are

A Piece on Doubt: These Waters

Watch a live performance of this spoken-word piece at:

hosannawong.com/interludes

I can trust God with my life
God has a plan for me
I was born with a purpose
I was born with talents
I was born with a mission
To see captives set free
I can trust God with my life

I'm trying to say these five truths
    to myself over and over
Hoping somehow they sink in
Praying somehow they shout
    louder than the voices that
    haunt me
Because from day to day they are
    battling
With all the wars inside of me
The many words inside of me
Like what if God fails me
What if I make a mistake
And I ruin the lives of the people
    around me
What if I'm the one person
Who doesn't have a purpose

What if my talents are not good
    enough
What if my decisions are not
    good enough
What if my life is not up to par
With what everyone expects of
    me
And I am drowning in a sea of
    what-ifs

But I am not the only one
I heard a story once
Of a man named Peter
Who was asked by Jesus
To come walk on water
Peter was at sea in a boat with his
    friends
A storm came in
And then Jesus from the shore
    began to walk on water
And then asked Peter to join Him
To take a leap of faith and step
    out with Him
Onto the waves beneath Him

Jesus asked Peter to trust Him
And for a moment, Peter did
And he stared into the eyes of
    Jesus
And he walked on water

But then his eyes got distracted
He saw the waves of the storm
He saw the ripples of the ocean
    underneath his toes
And then he began to sink in the
    sea of what-ifs

What if I can't do this
What if my feet slip
What if I don't make it
And I'm just a disappointment
What if I shouldn't have listened
    to Jesus

And the moment he looked away
    from Him
The moment he started to doubt
    Him
Peter began to sink in the sea
    that surrounded him
But Jesus reached out to him
Grabbed his hand and saved him

And said to him, "My friend,
    where is your faith?
Why would you doubt Me?"

And to be honest
The story isn't too different from
    me
See there's a little bit of Peter
Right here within me
There's a little bit of this lack of
    trust
Manifesting within all of us
Because we stop staring into the
    eyes of Jesus
And start looking at how scary
    the water is beneath us

But Jesus wants us to step out
To stop drowning in this sea of
    doubt
And start to walk on this water
He wants us to dive in
Into all His kingdom has to offer
And Satan has come
To plant doubt into our hearts
But Jesus has come
To redeem the what-ifs, and He
    wants to ask us

What if you just trusted Me with
   your life
What if you knew that I would be
   with you
When it comes to that high dive
What if you knew
These waters have been made
   for you
To walk onto
To dive into
And I would never let you drown
I am always here to catch you
What if you knew
You could trust God your Father
You could do even greater things
Than simply walking on water

See I know that doubt is
   comfortable
I know that doubt is all we know
I know that thinking
Of being loose from its chains
Seems a task impossible
But Jesus has come to pull us out
So that is the victory I hold on to
When demons of disbelief
Come back around and try and
   haunt me

When I start doubting like Peter
And I'm scared of drowning
I will stand with my head high
And stare my Jesus straight into
   the eyes
And take a step
And repeat and repeat and
   repeat all of this

I can trust God with my life
Because God has a plan for me
And I was born with a purpose
I was born with talents
I was born with a mission
To see captives set free

What if
What if
What if
I just trusted God with my life

There are no waters that are too
   deep for me[1]

How (not) to Save the World

#4 | Wait for Perfect

I downsized my life into two suitcases, threw them in my car, and had
no idea what I was doing.

Four years before this pivotal point, it seemed like everyone else
at my small Christian college had a clear idea of what they wanted to
do with their lives from the get-go.

"I want to be a pastor."

"I want to be a recording artist."

"I want to be a missionary overseas for at least ten years, then start
a school to train missionaries in the States for ten years, then plant two
more schools after that for the next ten years."

Amazing.

I had no such plans.

It's not that I lacked ambition. I lacked direction. I didn't know
where I wanted to live, what was left for me back home, or what
kind of career path was even possible for me. I felt like a five-year-old

with insufficient answers for the excited adults asking me what I wanted to be when I grew up. Astronaut? Doctor? Ballerina? I still have no clue.

So I didn't get involved in anything. I signed up for zero clubs. I volunteered for no events. I was intimidated by the myriad ambitious students with their thought-out plans and vegan-leather-bound journals of dreams, bucket lists, and projected timelines.

The world of Christian college is bizarre. There is a lot of outreach to be done, so ministry becomes as competitive in Christian schools as football is at the University of Michigan (Go Blue!). The head of the worship team is the quarterback. His swooning, cheering section is equally as obvious. The unpopular kids may not be Ally Sheedy in *The Breakfast Club*, hiding behind badly cut bangs and sitting alone in stairways, but rather those with less-holy ambitions or less-spiritual Saturday nights.

The first guy I dated in college was winning awards for his art.

The second guy I dated was en route to being a missionary.

Me? I was achieving . . . probation for drinking at parties.

I didn't know where I was going or what I was doing, so instead of going to the possibly wrong place, I was spinning in a merry-go-round of mediocrity, successfully arriving nowhere.

As each year passed, I realized that, though many students had seemingly more direction and far more impressive ambitions, they, too, were waiting for perfect. There were those who said, "I want to be a youth pastor after college." But when asked where they were volunteering to help young people today, they weren't—they hadn't yet found the perfect spot. There were those who said they wanted to lead worship in churches after college, and when asked where they attended church now, they hadn't yet found a place where the teaching matched their preference or the worship style was what they were looking for—they hadn't yet found the perfect situation. They were waiting for graduation to start saving the world.

We had all taken a number and were sitting in the waiting room for perfect. Our needs were simple: The perfect boyfriend or girlfriend. The perfect job. The perfect opportunity. The perfect class schedule. The perfect offer. The perfect church that had the perfect pastor (who told just enough jokes, but not too many) and the perfect service size, with the perfect small groups (who reached out enough, but not too much) and the perfect service times to accommodate our schedules . . . perfectly. *Come on, churches, how hard is that?*

For many of us, our fear of not being flawless stopped us from trying new things and even taking first steps. We dreaded the possibility of sending our lives down an irrecoverable road of defeat, with Siri unable to reroute us. We awaited the day when full clarity of calling would arrive and our lives had the straight-shot map to satisfaction and success. And wait we did.

This wasn't exclusive to my college experience. I've lived most of my life in fear of not making the *right* step. Even when I've actively been reading God's Word, talking with Him, and serving Him, I have been so afraid that I could take a wrong step and derail His entire plan. What if I heard Him wrong? What if He can't fix what I break? Preferring to be almost anything other than a failure, I have lived a lot of my life opposite of my hero, Mrs. Lee. I have shut doors and left tables.

But throughout the years, I have learned this: Waiting for perfect? That's how (not) to save the world. The lie that our next step must be perfect will stop us from taking any steps at all.

Have we become so obsessed with perfection that we've resorted to becoming a community of Christians who would rather do nothing? Are we so terrified about not singing a song perfectly that we'd rather not sing at all? That we'd rather not share our lyrical melodies with anyone? That we'd rather hoard what God has gifted us with until *we* deem it worthy? Have we become so afraid of not choosing the *right* church to attend or the *best* ministry to serve that we're not attending or serving at any? Are we living in so much worry of what other people will say of our start-up business, our unfamiliar endeavor, our risky idea, or the all-consuming passion that's burning within us that we let our light fade until the flame is the appropriate amount of heat that people deem acceptable?

Have we become a community of faith without any faith, holding back our engagement, silencing our songs, and extinguishing our fires, forfeiting in fear? Have we become a community of faith without any faith, shying back from starting anything until we know the end results? Have we become a community of faith without any faith, worshipping the perfect callings instead of the Perfect One who called us?

Hello. That is the foolproof way to fulfill none of God's purposes, to stay safe, spiritually dead, and increasingly ineffective. God has a better way.

I SAID, "BRUSH," KID!

I asked my nieces, Eden and Gracie, to grab me a brush for their hair before I told them a story and put them to bed. Without hesitation, Eden raced into the living room and hurried back with a purse. Gracie came stomping in from the same room with her mother's phone. I stood up and yelled at them until they cried, as they were in direct defiance of what I had demanded.

Just kidding.

They didn't fully hear me. They brought what they thought I said to bring.

I was impressed with how fast they went, and it did not remotely ruin our time together. I could still brush their hair before bed because I knew how much longer they could stay up and that I was in no hurry to leave. I also found a comb inside the purse Eden brought me, and we were able to FaceTime my mom, their grandma, with the cell phone. Ultimately, the brush was part of something I wanted to do *for* them and a way we could spend some time together, and that was still accomplished. Also, not to brag, but I was able to get the brush all by myself. (I know, right? Amazing.) Instead, this was better. They participated in the activity with me, the details in the middle were of little importance, and now I could tell them a story while combing their hair.

God knows when we think He said something. He knows when we took a step because we thought He was directing us somewhere. He knows the actual intention of our hearts. God's grace, patience, and love for us is so much greater than even what we have for those we love the most.

I am fairly certain that at the end of my life, when I see Jesus face to face and we're flipping through the seven millionth scrapbook of the snapshots of my life, there will be situations in which I'll say, "Whoops, I really thought you said to do *that*." And I fully expect my Friend and Savior to smile, perhaps chuckle, and say, "I know you thought that, Hosanna, I know." That's the grace I live in. He knows when I'm listening to Him and obeying Him as best as I can.

I am encouraged by the apostle Paul, who told the church in Rome that "God is able to orchestrate everything to work toward something good *and beautiful* when we love Him and accept His invitation to live according to His plan" (Rom. 8:28). As I truly love God and actively live according to His ways, He is able to use every step I take and choice I make and put it toward something good and *beautiful*.

The hard truth is that He really does know the motives of my heart. So even if I do something seemingly holy in the eyes of spectators but have a defiant heart toward Him and His leading, He'll also know (1 Cor. 4:5; Heb. 4:12–13). That neither pleases nor glorifies Him.

The wonderful, freeing truth is that when I feel Him directing, I don't have to wait for perfect, but I can go where I think He's leading and obey what I think He is saying.[a] Sometimes I'll even get it right. But every time I step out in faith to obey, trust, and rely on Him, He loves that. He'll use that. And ultimately, either way, we get to spend that time together. It was never about the brush anyway.

FAITH AS STRONG AS TOYOTA COROLLAS

I didn't do college perfectly, but I finally made a decision. *I may not know what to do, but I won't do nothing.* I remembered what I learned as a little girl, to be aware of gaps and seek to fill them. I volunteered at a tutoring program in a low-income neighborhood. No, I didn't know if I'd be a teacher one day, but I was doing something I believed in. I drove over an hour to perform spoken-word poetry at secular poetry slams on weekend (more on this in the next chapter; get excited). No, I didn't know if I'd be a professional performer one day, but I was doing something I enjoyed. I worked to be a better friend—I wasn't a great one at the beginning of college (after losing my dad my freshman year of college, I was angry and bitter toward many). Toward the end, I loudly supported my friends' projects and attended as many of their

---

a. God is never tugging at our hearts to do something that is not in line with His Word. Not sure if something aligns with His Word? Read His Word more. God is good, trustworthy, and consistent. (So, no, this section is not permission to disobey your parents and date that one boy.)

sports games, plays, and open mic events as possible. Even if I didn't know the perfect thing to do, I would do something.

Four years of college were now coming to a close, and I finally had the perfect plan. *Hooray! I did it!* Had it been the '90s, I would have raised the roof.

I was renting an apartment with my two best friends, becoming a full-time English teacher at an inner-city private school while also taking a bonus part-time job as a junior editor for a fashion magazine. After all those years of uncertainty and filling gaps where I could, I was finally seeing the flicker of a finish line.

Then God changed everything.

I received a call from an out-of-state camp director, and he offered me an opportunity to perform spoken-word poetry five nights a week for the ten weeks of their summer programming, starting the week after graduation. He said, "You won't make money, you'll have to work harder than you've ever worked in your life, but I'll let you on our stage, and you can be a part of life change."

I confidently said, "No, I already have plans after graduation, but thank you." He said, "I'll give you three days to change your mind." It truthfully didn't make sense for me to go, as I had no experience working with students or camps and no desire to. This yes didn't line up with my plans or my personality. And yet this was the first thing I thought of those three days and the last thing I thought of each night. I could barely sleep and would tear up praying for God to help me forget that phone call, as finals were overwhelming and this pull in my chest was leaving me with very few hours of rest.

What I didn't know at the time was that at the end of my summer at that camp, I would feel a similar pull on my heart once again, to not return home but to instead start traveling the country, telling the story of Jesus through spoken-word poetry indefinitely.

It was never only about the camp.

Three days later, he called again, and without a perfect plan or any idea of what the future might hold, I said yes.

Downsizing my life into two suitcases, I reluctantly rummaged through my closets, tossing my favorite blazers, refurbished vintage boots, and thrifted dresses to the floor. I had grown passionate about repurposing clothes and had hemmed, sewed up, and switched out buttons on quite a collection of special secondhand finds. I now had closets bursting with years of one-of-a-kind investments, the aroma of mothballs seeping through my drawers and bright-yellow sales tags sticking out of stacked cardboard boxes. My heart sank as I realized I couldn't take it all with me. (Some of you may think it's a bit dramatic that I would mourn letting go of such materialistic things. Maybe it was. Others of you are in deep pain wondering what happened to all those vintage dresses. Thank you. You're my people. We will heal together.) There was simply not room in my limited suitcases or in my 1996 red Toyota Corolla that would drive me across the country. (Don't hate on Corollas. Your great-great-grandma's Corolla still works and will never die. They're very practical and also dope. Take your judgment elsewhere.) I realized that if I was going to say yes to what I felt God was calling me to do, there were some things I had to be rid of. There was neither room for all my beloved material things nor my insistent need for perfection. Some things had to go.

I drove across state lines with fewer things and less certainty than I had ever felt in my life.

TIDE(S)

On the side of a highway, in the middle of nowhere, I came across a laundromat. To this day I could not tell you where this is. I didn't know the next time I'd be able to do laundry, so I pulled over. I may have been embarking on a bit of a hippie era, but rest assured, your girl was still going to be clean.

I sat on top of a dryer, the smells of lavender Tide detergent and sea breeze fabric softener swirling around me. I pulled out my janky laptop that could not run unless it was plugged into an outlet.[b] With the longest cord that's ever been recorded in all of cord history stretched across an otherwise empty laundromat, and with fear surging in my heart, I typed up what would become the opening lines to my spoken-word piece "These Waters": "I can trust God with my life. God has a plan for me. I was born with a purpose. I was born with talents. I was born with a mission to see captives set free. I can trust God with my life."[1]

I repeated the words to myself, hoping I'd start to believe them. I was reminded of Peter, who took a step of faith onto the crashing waves of the Sea of Galilee to walk toward Jesus but grew so consumed with doubt that he began to drown. I could relate. I felt like I was being capsized by storms of fear myself. I wrote that spoken-word piece as an anthem for my soul, declaring that I would keep my eyes focused on Jesus and walk confidently into the unknown. *I can trust God with my life.*

Over a decade later, I vividly remember that moment in the laundromat as if it happened days ago. At the time I thought, *I don't want to be like Peter. I don't want to doubt. I don't want to fear.*

> **I can trust God with my life.**

Now? I think that Peter gets a bad rep.[c] I always thought of him as a habitual doubter. He was the guy who was so overwhelmed by the

---

b. Definition of *janky*: to' up from the flo' up.

c. *Rep* is short for (a) *reputation* (e.g., "Jesus had a bad rep among the Pharisees") or (b) *representation*, *represent* (e.g., "I rep for my city" *throws Golden State Warriors jersey on*).

waves of his life that he lost sight of Jesus! He's the model of how *not* to live. *God, don't let me be like Peter!*

And yet Peter was the only one who got out of the boat in the first place.

Throughout all of Scripture there is no story of another human being trusting Jesus so much that they stepped out of a boat, stared into His eyes, and stepped onto the water. Yes, eventually Peter was distracted. Yes, when he lost sight of Jesus he began to drown. Yes, there's great lessons in that: we shouldn't be distracted, and we shouldn't stop staring at and focusing on the person of Jesus. All of that is *very* important. But this lesson from Peter is incomplete.

Imagine this. Peter throws his legs over the wooden boat to step out onto the body of liquid, his cloak weighing heavy as it starts to soak from the conquering waves. With every inch he sinks, his toes grow numb and his legs arctic cold. Jesus races the raging waves, reaching to grab His friend's slippery, shivering hands, strong-arming him up. One man drenched in salt water, with seaweed dragging from his ankles, and the other mostly dry with some of His friend's soaking garments dripping on His own, they link arms as if in protest of the dangers ahead and march forward together, heading back to the boat.

Who do they meet there?

All of the disciples who stayed safely inside the boat.

Perhaps they embraced Peter and gave him a cotton blanket to keep warm, comforting him from this trauma. If they were anything like we are when we see someone take a risk and seemingly fail, they may have made fun of him. They may have said, "We can't believe you went out there! What were you thinking?" Or "We were watching from here and laughing our heads off, saying, 'We knew it! There he goes, sinking!'" We have no record of what the other disciples said to Peter. But we know what we say to people who are trying something new and scary. More than that, we know what we envision other people saying to *us* when we're the ones heading out on a daring adventure. And for many of us, that's reason enough to stay in the boat.

What if they laugh and say, "I told you so! That was never going to work"?

What if they're disappointed and say, "Look at the mess you made"?

What if their pity grows condescending, and they say, "Aw, that was so cute that you tried"?

For some of us, our fear of the critics stops us from stepping toward Christ.

It didn't stop Peter. He had a faith in Jesus that was so strong that he did what none of his friends were doing. Like any of us who have taken a risk and a step toward Jesus, even while afraid, at one point he had doubts. He fumbled his footing. But then Jesus rescued him. Peter became the only person with the story of what it was like to walk on waves with his friend Jesus.

I used to believe the lie that I had to wait for the perfect situation to say yes to God. To have zero fears and zero doubts. To be the perfect age. To have the perfect team to come alongside of me. To have the perfect resources. Maybe you can relate. Perhaps you've felt the need for

- a more put-together home before having your neighbors over for a barbecue,
- the perfect understanding of the Bible and the perfect answers to everybody's questions before hosting a Bible study,
- the best and most expensive equipment before starting that one podcast or recording that one song,

- the most equipped volunteer team with the most impressive vision before volunteering on any team at all, or
- guaranteed amounts of resources and staff for a ministry or project you've dreamed of, instead of starting small where you are.

How many of us are waiting for the tides to settle, for the storms to calm, for the sky to be clear, and consequently are not getting out of the boat at all?

Do we know who it is who calls us?

Do we know He who calls us also rescues us?

Jesus-followers: Where has our faith gone?

We are assured in the holy Scriptures, "He has delivered us from such a deadly peril, and he will deliver us again. On him we have set our hope that he will continue to deliver us" (2 Cor. 1:10 NIV). The earthly waves are no reason to fear. God will never grow tired of rescuing us. The truth is that we're safer than we've ever imagined—to risk, to embark, to take a step of faith.

It's easy to make fun of Peter when you're safe inside the boat. It's easy to critique the players sweating it out on the field when you're sitting in the shade on the bench. It's easy to judge the singer laying her heart onstage when you're secure in the stands. (By the way, we must cheer on the Peters, the players, and the singers in our lives. It's not easy when a bunch of us haters are evaluating their every move.)

> **We don't want to aim for easy. We want to aim to be obedient.**

It's easy to be a critic when you're not doing anything that someone could critique. We don't want to aim for easy. We want to aim to be obedient.

At the end of my life, when I'm sitting around a campfire with my grandkids, telling them stories of a life lived alongside of Jesus Christ, may I not have a storybook of tales of all the times I stayed inside the boat. May I have no poetic portraits of what the dark-brown wood looked like and what the warm blankets felt like in all the safe vessels I sat in. May I have no memoirs of my distant view of all my crazy friends with crazy faith who leaped from the boat and what *their* lives were like. May I have some waves on me. May I have some stories of faith so daring that only Jesus could rescue me if I slipped. May I be able to tell them of a Savior who is bigger than they've ever imagined, who will be beside them with every single step.

Now that I've taken some risks in my life, fumbled a lot, sank a lot, and have been rescued by Jesus' saving hands . . . a lot . . . I no longer look down on Peter. Now I say: May we step out like Peter. May we risk like Peter. And whenever we doubt or slip like Peter, may we be rescued like Peter. May our lives tell the story of a Savior who loves us, calls us, and rescues us again and again.

For the record, when I do one day sit around that warm fire with my grandkids, roasting s'mores around the flickering flames and licking the melting Hershey's chocolate off our fingers, I know I'll tell them: "Every cold, crashing wave was worth it. Every laughing friend in the boat was worth it. Every quick grab of Jesus' saving hands was more miraculous than the last. And I hope everyone alive experiences the joyous thrill of stepping out in faith, the sensation of sinking, followed by standing amid storms with Jesus."

NEXT

As I finished writing my new spoken-word piece on top of the dryer and closed my computer, all of a sudden, multiple bookings, places to stay, a team of people, and big contract opportunities started coming my way.

Just kidding.

They didn't.

I fought back tears as I wound up my colossal computer cord, threw my now-clean laundry into my suitcase (not at all folded and embarrassingly imperfect), and tossed everything into the back of my (cool) Corolla, with about five more hours to drive. I didn't know what would come next, but I was taking the next step.

> We want to wait to say the *perfect* yes. Jesus is just asking us to say the *next* yes.

For some of us, we want to wait to say the *perfect* yes. Jesus is just asking us to say the *next* yes.

- Maybe your next step is writing a blog post. Before figuring out the perfect way to brand it or who exactly will read it or when the perfect time in life is to start it, friend, maybe your next step is writing the first post and clicking *Share*.

- Maybe your next step is telling a friend, "I have an addiction. I need help. Will you help me?" I don't know what your twentieth step will be, but maybe your next step is to get honest with one person who will come alongside you and journey the road to recovery with you.

- Maybe your next step is tithing to your church. Maybe you haven't been sure where God is calling you next or what areas you can partner with Him on His mission, but you know that where you invest your treasure, your heart will come more alive for that place (Matt. 6:21). Maybe your next step is telling your spouse, "Let's actively give more resources to our church together and see what God does in us and through us."

- Maybe your next step is to invite a group of neighborhood kids to play basketball on the weekends. You've always wanted to reach and mentor young adults but didn't know what kind of ministry to start. You've seen the expanding youth movements online and don't know how to begin to match those, but there's a basketball court at the end of your block and lots of students in your neighborhood with no big-brother or big-sister figures. Maybe your next step is inviting two high schoolers to shoot some hoops with you on Saturday.

Don't be overwhelmed with fear of not making the perfect step. Just take the next step. The next step toward Jesus. The next step of obedience. The next step of faith.

MY IMPERFECT JOURNEY

It was a good thing I didn't wait for perfect because perfect never came. I would soon cut up pieces of brown paper grocery bags and borrow markers from the youth camp's craft corner to create my first business cards. I handed them out to youth pastors if they saw me perform, in case they ever wanted to have me at their church. Some of the camp staffers laughed as I made them. But two gracious girls sat with me and helped me. More than forty pastors kindly declined and wouldn't take a glamorous card.[d] But eight did. Three of them invited me to their church that fall. It wasn't perfect. But it wasn't nothing. I cut up more bags.

I would soon record my first poetry CD at a church that allowed

---

d. So weird that a brown-paper-bag business card with the red letters SAFEWAY written across the back didn't scream "professional artist." Bizarre . . .

me to use their worship team's recording equipment for two hours. The creative arts pastor sat in the sound booth and recorded each track for me. He let me borrow the church's CD duplicator that could make five CDs at a time. I learned an off-brand version of Photoshop and watched YouTube tutorials showing me the dimensions of how to make a CD sticker. I would sell those CDs for five dollars each at conferences next to more legit artists with towering banners, professional photos, and sweet loading gear with band stickers.[e] Some of them looked at me and my table, turned, and walked by, clearly not interested in speaking to me. Some of them hung out with me and spent extra time encouraging me, and some I'm still friends with. It wasn't perfect. But it wasn't nothing. I duplicated more CDs.

When I made my public Facebook page, I was embarrassed about what my friends would say. It took me weeks to gather the guts to invite anyone to that page, knowing it would reveal the embarrassing small venture I was beginning. Some people accepted my invitation. Some didn't. Perhaps some people made fun of me. I don't know. It wasn't perfect. But I was taking a step. A new friend I met on the road at a conference knew how hard it was for me to put my ministry out there and wrote me a card and gave me flowers when I passed one hundred likes on my Facebook page. That might sound silly. It was. And it was also really comforting to have found a friend who was watching me fumble my way through and was with me in it, celebrating any victory at all, no matter how small it was to anyone else.

When I explained to people back home what I was setting out to do, I felt like a joke, and my heart felt hurt I didn't know it was capable of feeling. Someone said, "Don't come crawling to me when

---

e. *Legit:* Often thought to be slang for the word *legitimate* but is less like saying "lawfully accurate" and more like saying "The real deal. The authentic thing. Really, really good." For example, chips and queso are legit.

you run out of money; you're doing this to yourself." Someone else said, "I can't believe you're throwing away your college education to be a traveling poet." And another someone said, "Your dad would be so disappointed in you."

At the time, I knew they might be right. I was not sure what I was doing. I was not sure if my dad would be proud. I didn't know when I would run out of money. There were times I cried myself to sleep at night, unsure if I'd really heard Jesus right, unsure if I'd made the right step, reciting the spoken-word "These Waters" to myself, asking Jesus, "You're going to take care of me, right? I can trust You with my life?"

There wasn't a model of how to do what I was setting out to do. There wasn't a *Traveling Nomadic Christian Poet for Dummies* book. There was no instruction manual. There was just me taking the next step based on what I thought Jesus was telling me to do. All I was doing was all I thought He said to do.

My friend, I urge you—forget the critics. They're not worth your devotion. Let loose the plan you've held tight to. It may be limited by your vision. Our plans are no match for God's. We have no idea the people we will become and the power of God we will see when we release our plans and step into His.

Stop waiting for perfect. Abandon the need for complete comfort. Open up your clenched hands and release to God everything you've held on to that has kept you from fully trusting Him. You may not know the whole plan. You may not understand every opportunity. You may be tempted to wait for the perfect yes. God just wants you to say the next yes. And rarely does that line up with popular opinion, our greatest preferences, or the values of the world. But stepping toward Jesus is worth it. And you are safer with Him than you've ever known.

DON'T WAIT FOR THE PERFECT STEP

just take the NEXT STEP

How (not) to Save the World

#5 | Only Do What's Been Done

My ex-convict, drug-dealing friends on the streets of San Francisco taught me the art of spoken-word poetry. Some also taught me the art of poker, but thankfully I only pursued one of those career ambitions.

Where I grew up, everyone spoke hip-hop. Whether through break dancing on scorching sidewalks, emceeing at school rallies, rapping at hole-in-the-wall clubs, performing poetry at competitions in closed coffee shops after hours, or painting graffiti along concrete canvases in abandoned alleys, many found their own way to express their story, their respect for their roots, their outcry for social change, their loss, their victory, and their truest passions. For us, art was a megaphone for the truth to be heard—living newspapers updating the headlines with our stories, spray paint, and poetry. The streets had a voice. You could hear it. You could feel it. You could see it. Though at times we may have felt broken down and beat, we could break that beat down to create something beautiful.

My friends would freestyle at busy intersections and in doorways on the corners of our neighborhood.[a] Even at eleven years old they'd invite me. Some called me "Lil' Dubb" (as in *W* for Wong), but most called me "Little Girl," as I was the preacher's daughter from the park down the block (and that's what my dad called me) and also one of the few children roaming the streets of our hood. To this day, that's what most of my friends in downtown San Francisco still call me.

They'd signal me over; someone would cup his hands around his lips, creating percussions to lay down the beat; another would join, adding cymbals through his teeth, together conducting an orchestra echoing on the surrounding parking meters and trash cans. They'd throw me questions as prompts, and I'd attempt to riff on . . . whatever kids my age thought about, really. Pretty much how I loved my breakfast and how I hated my homework (deep stuff, clearly). Why they invited a little kid to join them, I'll never know. I wasn't very good, but as I got older, I improved. Eventually they'd start giving me faster beats and throwing me more serious prompts: "If you could change one thing about the world, what would it be? Go!" Hands cupped. Beats dropped. It was the best symphony in town.

While seeing difficult things at an early age muddled my mind, freestyling got me out of my head and helped me process many things out loud. Through free-versing, I discovered more about myself and what I had inside of me. The term *spitting rhymes* or *spitting poetry* comes from the very real, physical spit that often comes out of the passion and speed of a performing poet or rapper, but it also holds a second meaning in the hip-hop community. Spit represents the dirt inside of you. *"Spit" it out.* Don't cover up the dirt. Reveal your real story. Whatever is honest—that's what we want to hear. When

---

a. *Freestyle:* On-the-spot, off-the-cuff improvisational lyrics; words recited with less structure, more stream of consciousness.

it came to truth, many people hid it, but the streets demanded you spit it.

I eventually fell in love with the specific art of spoken-word poetry. Memorized oral storytelling with rhythmic punchiness, I like to describe it as a marriage between the styles of Anne Shirley and Tupac. It can be dramatic or comedic. Like most poetry, sometimes it rhymes, sometimes it doesn't. It can be spoken with speed, like a tongue twister taking over a town, or shared slowly and sweetly, like the final words a grandfather gives to his grandchildren during his last moments, the seconds both somber and sacred as he seeks to make sure they remember every . . . single . . . word. At its core, spoken word is poetry meant to be proclaimed. It's composed for the stage as opposed to the page. Unlike written poetry, spoken-word poetry must be heard in order to be experienced. If one-dimensional poetry is when the words are in you, two-dimensional poetry is when the words are on paper. Spoken word is poetry in person—storytelling in 3D.

I would write my words on cyan-lined notebook paper, scribble out the lesser prose, and rewrite, rewrite, rewrite until it was time to memorize, rehearse, and then perform these poems in public. I would perform these pieces in the Bay Area's local open mics held in record stores, delis, community college cafeterias, coffee shops, and tiny art studios tucked away in alleyways. I had a calendar on my wall of what nights venues allowed performers eighteen and under and would plan accordingly. Eventually, I would actively compete in the city's underground slam-poetry scene.[b]

---

b. A poetry slam is a competitive spoken-word poetry event, traditionally in front of a live audience and a panel of judges. Typically, an open mic is not competitive. Poetry slams are by definition competitive. You can be a spoken-word artist who does not compete and only performs at events without judges or scoring. However, a competitive spoken-word artist would be considered a slam poet. In most competitions, there are multiple rounds.

As with any artistic genre, every artist has their own style. Mine had natural rhythms of both declarative preaching and descriptive poetry interwoven by personal stories. Between hearing my dad preach and my closest friends freestyle, this combination was seamlessly becoming the natural language of my soul (but in a way less cheesy way, you know, a cool way . . . the natural language of my soul, *yo*). No one else in my family did it, and no one in my school did it. It certainly wasn't as impressive as my sister's singing or as powerful as my dad's preaching, but I couldn't do those things. Of course, I hoped to *eventually* be good at something that mattered. But in the meantime, this was my hobby. This wasn't ministry, this wasn't purposeful, this was just what I enjoyed.

The first time I wrote a spoken-word piece about Jesus, it changed my life forever. It came out of the overflow of my heart, from the natural (cool) language of my soul. I shared about what I was going through—my questions and my hurts, my sixteen-year-old declarations. As my personal relationship with Jesus was becoming more real, He was naturally seeping out of my spoken stories. I performed this piece at an outdoor event in our neighborhood, and much to my surprise, my friends gathered around the city block to hear me and sat to listen. What was happening? I fought to focus on not fumbling, but my inner thoughts were scrambling. Were my small spoken poems reaching people *for Jesus*? I had never seen that done before. Did sharing the gospel through poetry count as ministry? Was this sacrilegious? Was this allowed?

Sometimes the judges are experienced poets themselves, especially at high-level competitions. But in the underground slam-poetry scene, judges are picked based on who raises their hand to the question, "Who has never been to a poetry slam before?" That way, slam poetry remains the voice of the people. If you can't relate and speak to the everyday person, who cares if the artistic elite think you're impressive? There's a message in there for preachers too.

My friends stayed. And listened. Afterward, they asked me questions about my story and questions about Jesus.

There was no voice from the heavens declaring, "Hosanna, this is what God is calling you to do!" It was so not that spiritual. But in that moment, my expectations completely changed about what God could use and what God would use to point people to Him. I realized that something I loved and enjoyed was revealing Jesus to those in my neighborhood in the language they already spoke. I figured, *If this works, I'll do it again tomorrow.*

And then I just kept doing it.

I learned something that day: Only doing what's been done? That's how (not) to save the world.

Where did we learn the lie that we must have a certain skill, particular occupation, or a specific title in order to reach people for God and step into His purpose for our lives? Who told us that? Who told *you* that? Is it something another human said, giving you the false assumption that God's list of things He can use is tiny and tedious, laminated and exclusive? Or have we told ourselves this lie? Have we looked at other people's awe-inspiring skills and their impressive impact we've deemed far out of our league and resigned ourselves to believe we are the supporters on the sidelines, cheering on the world's best players?

If we believe these lies, we will miss the pivotal ways God wants to uniquely and powerfully use us. If we believe the truth, it will set us free and help us point others toward freedom too.

The truth is that we have been handmade by God to accomplish His good works (Eph. 2:10) and have been called to use every gift we've received and every skill we have for the good of others (1 Pet. 4:10–11). The things you love, the things you care about, the things you're passionate about, and the things you're good at: God wants to use it all. He's very eco-friendly like that. He doesn't waste one thing. Whatever you give Him, He'll use. The details of our lives that we have neglected may be the same details needed to carry out God's work.

It is a massive loss to the world when you don't use exactly who you are and what God has given you to reveal to the world how amazing He is.

It's a sad day when you stare at what all the people around you are doing and strive to be replicas of them, without pausing to consider what passions God has placed inside of *you* and asking God to reveal what gaps *you* can specifically fill. What if who you are and how you think is exactly what will reach people in your neighborhood in ways others can't? When we spend our time only focusing on what other people are doing and not what God is calling us to do, we are missing out, and so is the world.

It's a sad day when you want to start a ministry at your church and you're planning it based on how you've seen this kind of ministry done in your home state twenty years ago, without considering the city you live in now and how you specifically can help meet the needs of the exact area you're in. What if the leader you are and the things you enjoy are precisely the right recipe for what God wants to do in the lives of those around you? When we're too busy obsessing over how other leaders have led, we are missing how God wants to use us to connect people to one another and to Him right now. We're missing out, and so is the world.

It's a sad day when you look at what everyone else's social media feeds look like and work to make your life look like someone else's. Maybe you don't feel your own city is as glamorous as theirs. Or your home is as well decorated as theirs. What if God wants to use your story, your perspective, and your real life to show other people how He can come into their real lives? Don't miss out on being the example you wish you had. Many of us have thought on the kinds of role models this generation needs, and it's time we stop hoping for it and start stepping up to be it.

The Enemy hopes we all do the exact same thing, look the exact same way, and use the exact same methods so we only reach the same select group of people. If we were to tap into our unique perspectives, talents, and callings, we'd reach more people for Jesus. We'd reach those who love to read blogs and those who prefer to watch short films. We'd reach people who love dogs and those who love cats. (Although, is there any salvation for cat lovers? I kid. Sort of.) We'd reach those in rural countrysides and those in the inner city. We'd reach CEOs in large companies and the kids freestyling on our street corners. If we were generous with our different perspectives and variety of talents, we'd reach more people. It's math.[c] Because of this, the Enemy of our souls hopes we never activate the gifts God has given us and we never step into our full purpose. The Enemy hopes we spend all our time copying and pasting other people's lives instead of living as the originals God created us to be.

Your lens during your lifetime is important. The story of Jesus may have been told, but maybe you haven't told it yet. God gave you the gifts needed to glorify Him and make Him known within your generation. Exactly who you are and exactly what you have is what God wants to use for this exact moment in time.

> Exactly who you are and exactly what you have is what God wants to use for this exact moment in time.

---

c. It *is* math.

Spoken-word poetry was not something I read about ministers doing one hundred years ago or something everyone else in my community was doing to tell the story of Jesus. At the time, I saw it as nothing more than a hobby. It was what I loved to do, what my friends on the streets enjoyed, too, and I worked hard on it. As my fellow artists taught me, I shared my most honest truths, and as Scripture taught me, I did it with all my heart—whatever I put my hands to, I worked to be excellent and to glorify God with the result (Col. 3:17).[d] And He used it. There's nothing so small or simple that it can't be used to show off God's glory.

I had no idea when I did this as a little girl that I'd still be doing it today. I had no idea that God would use a childhood hobby to become a weapon to fight for His people.

GUNG HAY FAT CHOY

My favorite Chinese New Year tradition is the passing out of tiny red envelopes. I won't assume that everyone reading this book is extremely familiar with Chinese New Year customs, so if you *are* familiar, go ahead and skip this section. If not, let me untangle the noodles.

This yearly custom is all about giving and receiving, bestowing honor, and building relationships. Bright, apple-red envelopes, typically decorated in gold-foil Chinese calligraphy, are passed around with money inside. (That's right. Bet you want to start celebrating with us, don't you?) Depending on where in China the family is from, the custom varies, but for my family, it was the married couples who

---

d. All translations of this verse are so good. One of my favorites is from *The Voice*: "Surely, no matter what you are doing (speaking, *writing*, or working), do it all in the name of Jesus our Master, sending thanks through Him to God our Father." No matter *what* it is, let it bless Him and bring Him glory!

gave the single individuals the crisp cash. This is a token of saying, "Happy New Year!" In Cantonese you say, "*Gung Hay Fat Choy!*" The enveloped gifts are a way of saying, "We have found good fortune, love, and success, and we hope to pass that on to you."[e] Amounts could be two dollars, ten dollars, or twenty dollars,[f] and after a large dinner of fried duck, wonton soup, baby corn, and lots of white rice, the beloved tradition would commence. As a little girl, depending on how many relatives were in attendance that year, sometimes my sister and I could leave with over forty dollars each! Amazing. The apostle Paul once wrote that staying single was preferable. (Perhaps he was Chinese.)

When my little brother, Elijah, was born, it changed everything. So far, all of the grandchildren and all of my cousins were girls. He was the first boy in the family since my grandparents came to America. Now, while my sister and I were being given two dollars or four dollars per envelope, Elijah, from birth, by Chinese tradition, was getting twenty dollars and fifty dollars in his. Even before Elijah could count, his pockets were ripping at the seams with those *dolla' dolla' bills, y'all.*[g]

But Elijah never spent his money. He had a ziplock bag full of his yearly New Year's earnings, and he hid it in a drawer, where it was left unused well into high school. Among the bulging bag was also years of gift cards given on birthdays and Christmases, Target, Starbucks, and Outback Steakhouse cards poking out of the now-worn plastic bag.[h] After every celebration, I'd watch Elijah go into his bag and add his gifts. He didn't want to use them.

---

e. I want to be clear that this is not a biblical, Jesus-centered practice. This is a cultural practice for the Chinese. Although, if you have an excess of resources, pass it on. That *is* biblical (1 Pet. 4:10–11).

f. The amount you receive depends on your relationship to the giver.

g. To translate: lots of dollar bills, everybody!

h. Outback Steakhouse is every little boy's dream.

I'm sure, as kids, my sister and I used our New Year's money to purchase mostly candy and cassette tapes, but as we got older, we invested our money into things we cared about. While my sister used hers to buy piano charts and I used mine to buy new journals, my brother hid his money away—the gift cards depreciating each passing year and the money left uninvested. He had more than we did, but what did it matter? He didn't use it.

Jesus told a story like this about a man who, going away on a trip, gave his servants various amounts of money as he headed on the road. He gave one $5,000, one $2,000, and the last $1,000. When he returned, he discovered that the first two had invested their money and doubled it! The one with one thousand, however, had buried it. In fear of doing something wrong with it, he chose instead to do nothing with the money.

The master's angry response is convicting. He said, "That's a terrible way to live! It's criminal to live cautiously like that" (Matt. 25:26 MSG).

Sometimes we live like this. At times we grow so fearful of doing something wrong that we opt instead to do nothing at all. Our fear of risking and failing becomes one of the Enemy's favorite roadblocks keeping us from fulfilling our God-given purpose. Instead of steps of faith, we prefer money-back guarantees.

It's noteworthy that the master gave each man an amount based on their own ability. The money wasn't a gift being distributed based on who was more valuable; it was a responsibility being *entrusted* based on that servant's specific traits, strengths, and weaknesses. What the master chose to do with his assets was not up to the servants. What was up to the servants was what they did with what they received.

We could have the best singing talent in the world, the most creative ideas for projects, the best strategies to build businesses, but if we don't use these skills, what does it matter? Someone with less natural talent in each of these areas who uses it, invests it, and is faithful with it will see more results than someone with a lot of skills who buries it.

You may feel like you don't have the skills other people do. You may not understand why some people were given opportunities that you weren't. You may feel like you don't have the title you ultimately want. The question is, What are you doing with what God has given you, and are you being faithful with it?

Jesus said, "Whoever can be trusted with very little can also be trusted with much" (Luke 16:10 NIV).

If you want to be used by God to accomplish His great work: Use what you have first. Invest what God has given you first. Serve where you are first. Don't just wait for something public. Don't just aim for something impressive. Be faithful with the little. Be faithful in secret. Who you are when no one is watching matters

> Who you are when no one is watching matters more than you know.

more than you know. And if you are ever given a bit more: the call is still to use what you have and be faithful.

POETRY & PANCAKES

In fear that doing something different would leave me in a heap of humiliation, there have been times I almost missed what God was calling me to do.

In high school, I almost missed it. Knowing I was the only student doing spoken word at my school's talent shows, I almost scribbled over my name on the bulletin board sign-up sheets.

After college, I almost missed it. That day in the laundromat where I wept in fear of what would happen next, I almost turned my car around and went back to the life that made me comfortable.

In my early twenties, I almost missed it. I had been performing spoken word on the road for over two years, but I was beginning to have weekends without work. I was living from host home to host home to Best Western (still some of the best oatmeal I've ever had in hotels, got to give credit where it's due) and on to another host home. And I had to be performing somewhere every week to make ends meet. *What do I do now? Do I give up? Is this the end? If God really called me to do this, then why aren't more opportunities chasing me down? If God is in this journey, then why is the next step not clear to me?*

The religious people during Jesus' time? They missed it. Trapped in traditionalism, their idea of Jesus was so specific that even when He actually came, they completely missed it. They missed Him. He didn't look like what they expected, far from what they envisioned, and though they were the ones most anticipating His arrival, they couldn't loosen their grip on their presuppositions.

It's a good thing that many men and women throughout history were not afraid to try something different. It's a good thing they didn't miss what was not yet but still could be created. The Wright brothers didn't miss it. Motor-operated airplanes didn't yet exist, but they imagined something they had not yet seen, took the risks, learned from their failures, and are credited for why we have air travel today. It's a good thing Rosa Parks didn't miss it. She dreamed of a world she had not yet seen, a world where every person of every race would be treated with equal respect and dignity, and she refused to sit in the colored section of the bus, sparking the Montgomery bus boycott. She took the risk, propelling nationwide efforts to end racial segregation, and was a key player in the Civil Rights Movement. It's a good thing Clara Barton didn't miss it. She saw a gap in the country's medical system and sought to provide aid to people in distress. She took the risks, did what she had never seen done before, and later founded the American Red Cross.

Just because we have not seen it yet does not mean it should not be done.

Just because it's different today doesn't mean it's not destined for tomorrow.

For many of us who have chosen Jesus, we are confident that He has the power to save us from our sins, from an eternal death, from our addictions, and from our shame.

> Just because we have not seen it yet does not mean it should not be done.

But we're not living like He can rescue us from making a risky career move. *He can save me from death. But can He save me from embarrassment?* Perhaps that's why our faith only goes so far. We want to obey God, we want to take a step toward what He's calling us to do, but we first need to know who else has done it this way, their success rates, the next ten steps after, the resources He'll provide, and the projected future outcome. Our actions show that we trust God . . . *sort of.*

With a couple of empty weekends scattered over the next few months, I changed my focus from what I didn't have to what I did have. There were families I had previously met on the road who had offered for me to stay with them the next time I was in their state. I could call and take them up on that. Each of those cities were places I had performed or spoken at before, and I knew of musicians and artists in each of those cities. With some creativity, nerve-racking phone calls, amateur graphic making, and planning, Poetry & Pancakes was born. (Going straight from college to road life, pancakes were the ceiling of my cooking abilities, plus I was on a strict budget. Little did I know, even those limitations God was going to use.)

The first Poetry & Pancakes event was in Avondale, Arizona. The last was in Kansas City, Missouri. Each night was filled with music, spoken word, community, connection, laughter, and lots of pancakes—with all the toppings you can imagine, from Oreos to sprinkles to gluten-free granola (yes, even those who are gluten-free are welcomed into the family of God). I didn't know what else to do, so I had to look at what I had. What abilities did I have? What resources did I have? What communities did I have? Was there anything I'd overlooked? It was easy to see what touring musicians were doing in vibey,[i] dark-lit venues and compare these small backyard events to theirs. It was easy to see what other events public speakers were putting on in refined rented halls and compare my quaint gatherings to theirs. I couldn't let my thoughts spiral. Perhaps my red envelopes weren't as filled as others, but I would use all I had.

God used it all. For the next couple of months, on once-vacant weekends between speaking at churches and conferences, dozens and then, before long, hundreds of people bought five-dollar tickets and gathered in backyards, living rooms, and massive driveways. At each event, people brought friends who said they would never step into a church building, but they were fine with coming to a night of poetry in a yard, underneath string lights, to watch a desert sunset or in a parking lot with folding chairs and blankets, lit up only by stars and flashlights on phones. On those nights, they experienced community, heard about Jesus, and ate fluffy, buttery pancakes. Friendships were made. Connections continued.

> Sometimes what looks like disqualifications may actually be doors to do something different.

---

i. *Vibey* is an adjective used when something gives off good vibes and creates a good mood. You might call it a bougie atmosphere.

It turns out that my limitations were not the end; they were actually the beginning.

Sometimes what looks like disqualifications may actually be doors to do something different.

YOU'RE IT

You are not merely an extra in the background of the supporting cast of the world, watching the main characters live out the more important roles. You've been divinely handmade and handpicked. The world needs Jesus. Somebody needs to tell them, and there's not a realm of superheroes from other various universes who are going to invade earth and fight the battle for people's lives for us (although a Jesus-centered Justice League would be awesome—dibs on the name Signs-and-Wonders Woman).

> Your details are your superpowers.

Jesus is the Savior, the One who saves lives, and He absolutely wants to use all the specifics He placed inside of you to show people who He is.

Your details are your superpowers.

- your quirks
- your story
- your scars
- your joys
- your hobbies
- your abilities
- your limitations
- your relationships
- your background

- where you're from
- what you've overcome
- what you're passionate about

Don't just look at what other people are doing or what's already been done in the past. You are uniquely created for such a time as this exact moment you are living in. What's the date on the calendar? What's the time? Check it. You were made for this moment, right now. Thank you for being here.

It's your availability on weeknights and funny personality that make your kid's friends want to come over and hang out at your house after school, giving them an example of a parent figure who is engaging, hilarious, and available.

It's your background going from foster home to foster home before being adopted that enables you to speak to people and listen to people with the same experience in ways that no one else in your community can.

It's your impressively long log of handwritten recipes and love for cooking that could help you start a Baking and Bible Study group where girls from around the community invite their friends and learn to bake together (clearly, that did not exist when I was a kid).

Hey, it may be your *inability* to bake, your *bad* singing voice, and your *lack* of financial resources that leads you to make pancakes, perform poetry, and only be able to do it in homes across the country. Yes, even our limitations are important and something God wants to use.

God has equipped us with everything we need to partner with Him on His mission. He just asks us to use what He's given us. Don't downplay it. Don't discard it. Instead, invest it, get creative with it, and be faithful with it. And then *expect* it. Be ready for when God does things through your life that you've never imagined.

Don't let your expectations become walls that stand in the way of what God wants to do in and through you. God may be calling you to break down barriers. God may be calling you to build what you've never seen built before. He may be asking you to grab a shovel, excavate tough soil, and pave a path where no road yet exists. He may be pulling your heartstrings to try something that does not yet make sense to you but absolutely makes sense to Him.

I promise you, whatever God wants to do, we don't want to miss it. Whatever He has given us, we don't want to bury it; we don't want to hide it; we don't want to ziplock it shut. Otherwise, the gaps in our world grow larger. The needs grow greater. And people all over the world continue to not feel seen, not feel heard, and not feel loved.

There's too much at risk.

Be who God has made you to be. Use what God has given you to use. Do what God has called you to do.

And then do it again tomorrow.

EXACTLY who you are & **EXACTLY** what you have *is what God wants to use for this* **EXACT MOMENT IN TIME**

How (not) to Save the World

#6 | Silence Your Story

The first Chinese woman I ever saw preach was me. For years I was not proud of my heritage and did my best to hide that I was Chinese. Though I'm confident many other Asian female speakers existed throughout the world, I had not yet seen them or seen an artist or Bible teacher on a conference bill with the last name *Wong*. It's hard to imagine something you've never seen before.

In my early years of performing spoken word on the road, I went by the pen name Hosanna Poetry. I did not use my last name publicly and did not speak of my family's background for fear it would stand in the way of the effectiveness of my ministry. I'm embarrassed to admit that I was afraid that being Asian would be a roadblock in my career. I thought my last name would be made fun of. I thought I would stand out too much. I saw what the other speakers—great people, my mentors and heroes—looked like, dressed like, and how they spoke, and I tried my best to fit what I presumed was the mold. Though I was speaking about Jesus as best and as truthfully as I could, I was working extra hard to leave the truth of *my* story out of it.

I was not raised to be proud of being Chinese. My grandma had a heartbreaking childhood in Kaiping, China, a city along the Tanjiang River, about 130 miles from Hong Kong. She came to America in hopes of a better life. Though we grandchildren celebrated traditional holidays like Chinese New Year and ate endless amounts of dim sum and bok choy, she told us not to learn the language. Whenever we talked about visiting China, she would drop whatever she was doing, look directly into our dark-chocolate eyes that looked just like hers, and say in her stern broken English, "Don't do that." I internalized the disdain toward the DNA that darted through my veins. Being multiracial, and Chinese only being one-half of me, I tried to bury that half as best as I could, learning how to do my eye makeup in such a way that made my eyes look bigger, spending more time on curling my lashes than tying my shoelaces before heading to grade school. I didn't want to be Chinese.

Miles McPherson calls this internalized racism. When someone "adopts the negative views and labels others have given them," it is the most difficult type of racism to protest because it's not outside of you—it's within you. "It impairs an individual's ability to recognize God's image in themselves."[1] I didn't need people to tell me I was less than. Deep inside, I already believed it.

I did not understand what it meant that I was made in God's image. *Does that just mean that God made me?* That part I understood. And yet I had always felt an internal sense that there was something flawed, inadequate, and second-rate about me.

There were also times I was ashamed of being my father's daughter.

Whenever we were invited to community events with other ministers and their families, I begged to stay home, trying to avoid the awkwardness amid the cliques of pastors' daughters I could never fit in with. I would conceal that our seats were mostly filled with our friends without homes and right out of prison, and I tried to pivot from any questions about the particulars of our ministry. It was clear their dads and their churches were not like mine. I didn't know why I was different, but I knew I hated it. I have a hunch my dad felt the same, as we would drive back home from these functions in silence. We did not fit in.

In eighth grade I went out on a date with a pastor's son in our community. Afterward his parents found me alone and told me that they did not condone us dating, that their son was going to be a pastor one day and I would hold him back in ministry. Without a team of backup to defend me, I stood there shaking, tearfully responding, "I'm also a pastor's kid; my family is also in ministry."

I'll never forget the mom's response. "Not the same kind of ministry. Our families are not the same."

All she did was confirm what I already felt deep inside of me.

I am not like everyone else. Something is wrong with me.

Years later, as I began to perform spoken word and share sermons, I worked hard on my biblical knowledge, double-checking my theology and doing all I could to reveal the truth about Jesus. Perhaps I worked just as hard at not revealing the truth about me, leaving out details about my background, my father, my heritage, my brokenness, my insecurities, and my deepest hurts. I was already insecure about being a female speaker, blaringly aware of how I stuck out among my peers, and I didn't want to highlight any more possible barriers. *The less like a woman I preach, the better. The less Chinese I look, the better. The less of my story I share, the better.*

With most of my heroes and mentors at the time being white male pastors, I studied their videos and tried to learn how to teach like them. I saw the type of stories they told and tried to think of stories in my life that were close to theirs. I learned how they told jokes and worked to mimic them. I learned amazing tools (and highly recommend that, in any field, you study from those more experienced than you), but at the time I was doing more than learning from and being inspired by them—I was trying to duplicate them. This was not solely out of insecurity. It was also what I was convinced I needed to do in order to be successful in my career and effective in ministry. I thought I needed to preach like the boys to be able to preach at all. Ironically, many of these same white men I looked up to and tried so hard to preach like later took me under their wing and said, "It's time to be who you were created to be. It's time to tell your own story."

> When you cover up who you are, you cover up God's design and God's power.

Degrading your details? Living in shame of who you are? Silencing your story? That's how (not) to save the world. When you cover up who you are, you cover up God's design and God's power.

It took me years to learn that being made *in God's image* didn't solely mean I was created *by God*. It's so much more. We first discover this truth in Genesis:

> Then God said, "Let us make human beings in our image, to be like us. They will reign over the fish in the sea, the birds in the sky, the livestock, all the wild animals on the earth, and the small animals that scurry along the ground."
>
> So God created human beings in his own image.
>
> > In the image of God he created them;
> >
> > male and female he created them. (Gen. 1:26–27 NLT)

We were not just handmade *by* the Creator of the universe like every other thing that has ever been created. Humans have been set apart from every other creature, made in what theologians call *imago Dei, the image of God.*

Simply put: God's own image is stamped on us and within us. Being made in the image of God means every man, woman, and child, regardless of ethnicity, race, or socioeconomic background, has intrinsic, built-in worth. Value flows through our veins. Dignity is in our DNA. No other created thing can take away what the ultimate Creator has designed us with. We already wear His image. This truth changes how we see ourselves and how we see others.

Jesus lived a life elevating the marginalized, declaring this dignity everywhere He went.

- Jesus elevated the least advantaged and society's outcasts. He proclaimed, "Whenever you saw a brother *or sister hungry or cold,* whatever you did to the least of these, so you did to Me" (Matt. 25:40).
- He elevated women. A woman named Martha invited Jesus into her home, "and she had a sister called Mary, who was also seated at the Lord's feet, and was listening to His word" (Luke 10:39 NASB). By sitting at Jesus' feet, Mary was taking the cultural posture of a disciple to a teacher. This would have been controversial at the time for a woman to sit like this, and yet Jesus did not dismiss her. Instead, He welcomed her.[2] As Martha argued that Mary should have been helping her to host, Jesus replied, "There is only one thing worth being concerned about. Mary has discovered it, and it will not be taken away from her" (v. 42 NLT).
- Jesus elevated marginalized groups and ethnic minorities, deeming them worthy even when they didn't deem themselves

worthy. Jesus spoke to a Samaritan woman at a water well in the middle of the day, asking her for a drink of water, then telling her who she was and the eternal life that was found in Him. Jesus even speaking to her was against multiple cultural norms, as Jews hated Samaritans, and men (from both cultures) would not speak to women like this in public. The woman knew this. She said to Jesus, "I cannot believe that You, a Jew, would associate with me, a Samaritan woman; much less ask me to give You a drink" (John 4:9). Jesus didn't disqualify her. She disqualified herself. *I can relate.* She later came to believe that Jesus was who He said He was. (By the way, this same Samaritan woman provides the first account we have of someone going out of their way to tell people of how Jesus personally changed their life.[3] Read John 4. She went and told her whole town. People came to know Jesus. Through someone many would dismiss. It's a good thing Jesus did not.)

- Then Jesus died for the sins of all humans, demonstrating how valuable every single one of us is to God. We were all worth Jesus dying for our sins so we could be united with God.

The disdain I had toward how I was created did not come from God. Jesus elevated those whom others denigrated. Over time, I learned these truths from the Word of God that I want to pass on to you. If you believe in the God of the Bible and that what He says is true, then

- you are made in His image,
- you not only have access to know Him but authority given by Him to make Him known, and
- you not only have the permission but the responsibility to use

who He created you to be, with the story you have, to glorify Him and carry out His mission.

FREEDOM IN ALASKA

In 2015 I spoke at a women's prison in Eagle River, Alaska. Not new to preaching in prisons, I wore no makeup, let my hair rein free in its natural state, and spoke as if this was these ladies' only chance to hear the gospel. Leaving my car keys, cell phone, and ego at the door, I shared about my father, my deepest insecurities, my greatest failures, and my sins that have hurt people the most. I wept as I told them of the freedom my father had found in Jesus, that I later found in Jesus, and how that same freedom was available to them, no matter what. I shared things I had never shared in public before in a large gym filled with inmates, some tightly chained to cold metal bleachers in the back of the room.

After I invited them to give their lives to Jesus, I was able to meet many of them. And it was through talking to these inmates who were living behind bars that I was beginning to be set free. Many of them had never heard a woman share the gospel before, and because of their previous hurts with men in their pasts, they hadn't been receptive to the story of Jesus from the previous speakers. Many of them (all of various races) commented on how I looked like them or their daughters or nieces and how they never saw someone who looked like them talk about Jesus that way. They spoke about their parents who were also battling addictions and the shame of their own sins—some of which they also had never admitted to anyone. They expressed their feelings of never fitting in and assuming God was far out of reach for someone like them. Until now. Dozens gave their lives to Jesus that day. They were no longer going to live in shame but were ready to start getting honest about who they were.

They were already bolder than I was.

I was convicted.

I had been so wrong.

Why had I been hiding my real story for so many years? Why had I hated the details of how I looked so much? Why was I so adamant about concealing what God really brought me through? Why was I ashamed of myself, someone created in the image of the almighty God? Why did I disdain His creation so much? Somehow, it was being a woman, multiracial, and the kid of a recovered-addict street preacher that helped me reveal the truth about Jesus that day. The things I wanted to hide were the things God wanted to use to expose who He is and what He can do.

> **The things I wanted to hide were the things God wanted to use to expose who He is and what He can do.**

I spent so much of my life trying to figure out who I was supposed to be like that I didn't realize I was supposed to be more of who I already was. I thought the details of my life were walls, but they were doors. These doors were helping me invite more people into the story of a redeeming Savior. I was choosing to keep them closed, but I didn't have to. God wanted to use my real story to reveal His real power. And He wants to use yours.

What has stood in the way of you sharing your story?

- Perhaps other people have told you the box you need to fit in, and you're exhausting yourself aiming to shape-shift into that mold, leaving out the true details of who you are.
- Maybe lies in your childhood have kept you from fully embracing

who you really are, and your shame has been a red light stopping you from moving forward in your purpose for your entire life.

- Perhaps you've internalized insecurities deep down, and though no one has told you "You can't," your own echoes of this lie ricochet in your mind with each passing opportunity. You haven't seen yourself as made in God's image. You haven't embraced the value of your story.

- Or maybe it's a fear of rejection deep inside of you that if people knew the real you, the full you, you would lose a status you've worked so hard to achieve.

All of these things have stood in my way too. And I don't want the Enemy to have victory through our shame or our silence any longer. Our stories are too important to be kept hidden. God's image must be seen, and His power must be exposed.

WITH

The bolder I became in sharing my story in churches and at events, the more I realized my experience was not exclusive to that one prison in the snowy mountains of Eagle River. Everywhere I went there were people—not who necessarily looked like me or had backgrounds like me—who felt they also didn't fit any mold around them and needed to know Jesus was available to them too, right where they were, no matter what they'd done or where they came from. They needed to know God's image was on them. They needed to know their life was important and their story had a purpose.

It turns out, people don't want to be impressed. People want to be seen. People want to be known. People want to know they are not alone.

People need to know that the Jesus they've heard of is not some unattainable, far-out-of-reach, cosmic fantasy. People need to know there is an actual, available Listener, Comforter, and Rescuer who will urgently meet them in their dirt, sit with them in it, carry them through the mud, and be on their side through their real life. When we hide the truth of the pit Jesus has saved us from, we hide the truth of the person and power of Jesus.

> People don't want to be impressed. People want to be seen. People want to be known. People want to know they are not alone.

So why are we keeping Jesus locked up behind closed doors, in the pages of our journals, in books never written, in sermons never preached, in songs never sung, and in stories never told? Why are we silencing our stories?

We know that God's mission from the beginning of time has been to be *with* us. We know one of the names of Jesus is Immanuel, meaning *God with us*. Yet so many of us are showing a Savior to the world that is *God way out there* and *beyond our reach*. We do that by being fake with the people around us, erasing the details of our real lives and putting on a theatrical show filled with grandiose costumes, facades, and memorized lines, living more to be *above* than to be *with*.

Pretending your life is perfect all the time does not show people how Jesus can be with them in the mess of their lives. Hiding the details of what Jesus saved you from does not show people how Jesus forgives, redeems, and restores anyone who receives His great invitation. And it turns out, preaching about the power of Jesus in people's lives without sharing about His power in your own life does not reveal the power of Jesus at all. Hiding my ethnicity, my battles with my identity, and my upbringing on the streets did not enable me to help people to the full capacity I could have. I was not showing people who I really was, who God really made me to be, or the brokenness He really healed me from. God did not want to use my fake story, written and curated by me. He wanted to use my real story, created by Him and cowritten with Him. God is a better author. And God wants to tell a better story.

> There is no point in putting on a facade to impress a world that Jesus has called you to serve.

God wants to use the real you. There is no point in putting on a facade to impress a world that Jesus has called you to serve. Instead of seeking to impress people, seek to impact people. In a world where many aim to appear *above* other people, aim to be *with* people where they really are.

KEEP LAZARUS ALIVE

One of the most notable (and just plain craziest) miracles recorded in the Bible is when Jesus raised His friend Lazarus from the dead. As Jesus was walking from city to city with His friends, having typical friend hangs—you know, healing people—religious people were out to get Him, lock Him up, be rid of Him, and, we know how the story goes, eventually kill Him. But Jesus was not the only one they sought to destroy. In fact, the religious leaders knew that killing Jesus was not enough to accomplish their plan.

What?!

People trying to kill Jesus is the climax to our Christian history, no?

From the second we enter Sunday school, cartoon Jesus is on the cross on a poster above the bright-blue-and-yellow cubby holes, and we are taught right away how the bad guys searched for Jesus, found Him, and killed Him. Then we are given Cheez-Its and the chance to watch VeggieTales! This is the primary plot point we have learned since we were four. Who else's death could *possibly* be important?

Lazarus.

The chief priests were secretly plotting to murder both Jesus and Lazarus, for his story was living proof that Jesus could raise the dead, and "on account of him many of the Jews were going over to Jesus and believing in him" (John 12:9–11 NIV).

They didn't want to just destroy Jesus. They wanted to destroy the proof of His power. They wanted to erase any evidence of what He could do. Everyone had heard that there was a man named Lazarus who was dead but now lived. Even without *People* magazine in their grocery store checkout lines and Twitter updates flooding their phones, news traveled fast, especially when it involved a funeral a bunch of people attended, and now that same dead guy was eating at a restaurant across the way. Lazarus was walking, indisputable proof. Even if they got rid of Jesus, *they'd still have to get rid of Lazarus*. Perhaps some people weren't sure about all the rumors about Jesus, the stories spreading around town that He could heal the blind and raise the dead, and hadn't yet decided what they thought about who He claimed to be. But then they saw Lazarus.

The story of Lazarus was a direct threat to everything the Enemy wanted to accomplish—to keep as many people as possible from the truth about Jesus. And threats to his agenda were popping up everywhere. This wasn't just about Lazarus. This was also about the blind who could now see. Those who couldn't walk now running in the streets. Every person once ill, outcast from society, who did evil things and had irrecoverable reputations now living healed, full lives. Everywhere people looked, there was living proof.

In *your* school, people may not be sure that God can come into their mess and fully redeem them from what they've done. But then they hear your story. There's living proof.

Your group of friends may not be convinced that they can be free from their anger and cynicism. But then they see how you don't gossip with them anymore, how you're more forgiving and even-tempered, and they begin to see that freedom is possible. There's living proof.

On *your* social media, in *your* community, and at *your* place of work, people may not be sure if the God they hear about has anything to do with their everyday lives. But then Haley walks in the room. Jim shares his story to his recovery group. Jada shares about how Jesus changed her life before singing a song she wrote at a talent show. Dharius is more encouraging than he's ever been. Selena is more honest than she's ever been. *You* are noticeably a different person, and it's pouring out of how you speak, treat people, and share about how Jesus has changed you completely.

The proof of Jesus' power lies in the telling of your story.

In Paul's words, "Your life story confirms the life story of the Anointed One" (1 Cor. 1:6).

This is no longer about Lazarus. This is about every single one of us.

> The proof of Jesus' power lies in the telling of your story.

Every person who was ever told that they were not enough and who lived as if they had no purpose, then found Jesus and started dreaming big dreams, taking steps of faith, and showing no fear of the opinions of man—they're the proof.

Every person who thought they'd never be free from their addictions, then found Jesus and stopped using substances or resorting to old habits to fill the void in their hearts, started leading groups, and helping others with their recovery—they're the proof.

Every person who was known for being divisive, gossiping, and tearing other people down, then found Jesus and started reconciling relationships and using their words to bring people together and build people up—they're the proof.

The Enemy wants you to keep your story hidden.

Keep Lazarus alive.

The Enemy wants you to pretend like you're perfect, have always been perfect, and never needed a Savior to pull you up out of the mud.

Keep Lazarus alive.

The Enemy hopes that you disdain how God designed you and conceal who God created you to be and what He has brought you through.

Keep Lazarus alive.

The Enemy could not keep Jesus in the grave. Don't let the Enemy have victory in keeping the proof of His power buried either. Keep the evidence circulating. Let your story be heard and keep Lazarus alive.

We must share the details. We must share our stories: lives that were dead are now raised, eyes that were blind now see. Our real stories are a real threat to the Enemy. The more people hear about the freedom you've experienced, the more they'll know about how free they can be.

Where can you start?

You can summon up the courage to share something you've never shared before with a close friend. Then you can take it even further. Share a part of your story that will take vulnerability and bravery with a small group of friends. Write a post on something God has done in your life and share it on Facebook. Film the video. Write the song. Go to the open mic. Start telling parts of your story to your coworker. Ask if you can share at your church's youth group. Pray for God to open more opportunities for you to tell the truth of your changed life to your community that doesn't know Him. It's amazing what happens when we ask God to open doors. Look for chances to reveal the real power of Jesus through your real life. Seek out and pursue opportunities to start more honest conversations.

Authenticity is one of the most contagious things in the world. You never know who may see the power of Jesus through the rawness of your story and be inspired to get real with theirs. The more you allow the details of who God made you to be and the truth of how He has saved you to seep out into your everyday conversations, the easier it will become, the more you'll naturally do it, and the more people will hear the full, whole, and healed life available to them.

I'm not saying that showing the world Jesus will be easy. *Not at all.* I'm saying it will absolutely take your participation. It will likely take these three things: making invitations, having conversations, and sharing your story. It will take your real life being revealed, your actual details being shown, and your true story being told. Too much is at risk for us to hoard this message. For as long as we live, may the proof of Jesus Christ be seen, heard, and kept alive.

How (not) to Save the World

#7 | Hide Your Faith at Home

My favorite job ever, besides being a preacher and a poet, was working at a Party City knockoff store in the hood. Though a less-clean, less-stocked, and less-organized version of our better-known competitor, our prices were the *tiniest* bit lower, and even ballers on a budget needed parties![a] I filled up hundreds of balloons with helium, stocked shelves with tiny Mardi Gras beads and larger-than-life Disney character Halloween costumes, and sliced open countless cardboard boxes with bright-yellow box cutters as if giving the new shipments open-heart surgery. (Except, instead of pulling out organs, we pulled out sparkly confetti.)

As is typical with most work environments, none of my coworkers were Jesus-followers yet. As we clocked in and clocked out together, spending hours stocking and selling celebratory supplies, I often

---

a. *Ballers on a budget:* ballers, who are bougie, but are also on a budget.

wondered: *How do I naturally bring up God without being weird? How do I represent Jesus well to people who might have a bad taste in their mouth about Him or a bad history with Jesus people? I also want to be friends with everyone . . . is there any way to do both?*

Have you felt this way at work or during your everyday social activities? In order to share Jesus, are my only two options to be abrupt and awkward, making sure I mention my faith as soon as I meet everyone, or to not be my true self, not talk about the most important relationship in my life, and try to have friendships with people without them knowing who I really am? The answer is no. Neither being aggressive nor evasive will allow us to have real relationships or point others to the most important relationship they could ever have. If our goal is for everyone to know they are loved, valuable, and that God wants to be with them, then neither hostile faith nor hiding our faith will reveal His real love to them. Though both options might be easier, neither will be effective. Hiding your faith at home? That's how (not) to save the world.

So far we've talked about making invitations, having conversations, and sharing our stories—opening the door, sitting at the table, and telling the truth. Now how do we practically implement all of that in our work and social lives? I've gotten this wrong oh so many times, so I want to share some truths I've discovered and, frankly, some things I'm still learning.

It can be easy to dismiss our work environments altogether as places to know people or reveal God's love to people. But that's a big mistake. Research shows us that one-third of our lives is spent working.[1] No matter if you're an engineer, teacher, coach, app developer, singer, construction worker, driver, manager, sales associate, or chief of helium balloons and fun for all at the party supply store,[b] our attitudes

---

b. Sure, "chief of helium balloons and fun for all" is a title I gave myself, but this book is in print now, so it's basically official.

toward our work and toward our coworkers *must* be important because they account for one-third of our one precious lifetime.

WISDOM IN THE WORKPLACE

Joseph's story in the book of Genesis gives us some great examples of how wisdom and excellence in the workplace opened many doors for him to serve God, serve others, and make God's power known. He was born into a family of hardworking shepherds, but his brothers sold him to slave traders who sold him to Potiphar, an imperial court official serving Pharaoh, the king of Egypt. There's much we can learn from Joseph's life, but as it pertains to his posture at work, I want to suggest four practices that will help us represent God well in our places of work.

Don't Be Entitled. Be Invested.

Even as a slave, Joseph didn't live entitled to a higher position; he invested in the position he was in. Over time, Potiphar promoted him to head of his household. I believe God wants us to be standouts in our fields. To be people of uncommon character in common workplaces. When people see something different in you, they become curious about the higher standard that you live up to. Many of us want the position, the power, and the influence, but few of us want to invest where we already are. Joseph showed us a better way.

Years passed, and Potiphar's wife tried to seduce Joseph. But like a track star hearing the starting shot, he ran from her. Even though he was a slave, and perhaps could have used favor from her to step up his status, he respected his position under Potiphar too much; he honored Potiphar and he honored God.

We may not have the exact same situations that we need to flee from, but we may have a chance to blame someone else for a project we dropped the ball on or to join in on crude, inappropriate talk in the workplace or to tell our boss we worked hours we didn't. Many of us have had opportunities to dishonor God, our bosses, and our co-workers, times that no one but God knows about. Here, Joseph showed us an example that we, too, can be people of integrity, honoring God and honoring others, even behind closed doors.

Potiphar's wife lied to her husband and said Joseph had tried to seduce *her*, which landed Joseph in prison. Even in prison the Lord's hand was on Joseph. He was a proven man of honor with an excellent work ethic, and then—plot twist—the jailer put him in charge of all of the prisoners.

The next episode of this Joseph show is a scene where the king's cupbearer and baker offend the king and are both thrown into the same jail. They have terrible dreams, and Joseph cares for them, asks them about their dreams, and seeks God to interpret their dreams for them.

Could you imagine a world where you go above and beyond in reaching out to the people in your workplace? Investing in people outside of the call of duty? What doors would that open? What would that say of you?

- What if you attended all the dinner parties your coworkers invited you to? What if instead of rolling your eyes, feeling like being around coworkers without being paid isn't worth it, you brought the best savory snacks and house gifts for the hosts and were fully present at every social event? I wonder what relationships that would grow.
- What if you intentionally scanned your calendar to see if you could cover for your coworker who is hoping to go on a trip?

What if instead of immediately saying no, not wanting to be inconvenienced in the slightest, and unsure of the ways they could repay you, you found a way to say yes? I wonder what your kindness would mean.

- What if you planned meal trains for your coworkers when they were on maternity leave, cleaned up shared spaces without being passive-aggressive, and were verbally thankful and uplifting to your coworkers, interested and invested in their lives? I wonder what type of environment you would create.

Eventually the cupbearer was released back into the palace, and Pharaoh had a dream. The cupbearer remembered Joseph, a man who was there for him in prison and interpreted his own dream once. Based on his experience with him, and based on Joseph's reputation, the cupbearer recommended Joseph be brought to Pharaoh. Joseph sought God to interpret the dream, and Pharaoh placed Joseph second in command in Egypt. Second only to Pharaoh.

As the great poet Drake once said, Joseph started from the bottom, now he's here.[c] But how did he get there? What was Joseph known for? What was his reputation?

His reputation was excellence.

Make Excellence Your Brand.

Make excellence the standard of quality that everyone knows will be stamped on any task they give you. Proverbs 22:29 tells us, "As for those who are skilled in their work, they will *be recognized and invited to* serve kings." That's literally what happened with Joseph, and that same principle applies to us. God does not want us to simply mirror

---

c. My own remixed version of Drake's "Started from the Bottom" hip-hop bop. A mixtape feat. Joseph.

the work ethic of what we see everyone else doing or to just do the bare minimum of what we've discovered we can get away with. No matter what line of work we're in or how temporary we might feel our job is, I believe Christ-followers can be the ones to set the bar and raise the standards for our coworkers, our industries, and our world.

My job at the discount party supply store might not have been my dream job, but over time I started treating it like it was. I set my alarm early to ensure I'd always be on time. When my boss asked who could stay later, I'd raise my hand whenever I could, and I tried to make it fun for other workers who stayed, bringing a small stereo to blast the latest hip-hop as we counted the latest shipments. Many relationships formed at our late-night inventory dance parties. When customers would complain about the balloons they wanted being out of stock, I would make it my duty to create other alternative balloon structures and color schemes to go with their theme in a creative way, and I did my best to create an environment of fun in the process. After all, *we were the party people!*

Some of us fall into the trap of merely *chasing* kings, saying, "When I work for a king, when I work for this person of influence, or when I work for a better boss, *then* I'll form new habits, *then* I'll care about work, *then* I'll really show up, *then* I'll care about having relationships with my coworkers."

The truth is that when you bring excellence to what you do every day, it attracts kings. Your boss. Your boss's boss. Owners of businesses. Those who know God and those who don't. They all want people to sit at their tables who are skilled and who care about their work.

Lead Before You're a Leader.

Many of us want the promotion, but we want to skip the process. Many of us want the recognition, but we don't want to own the responsibility. Joseph did the opposite. He led without the title. When he was put second in charge of all of Egypt, he already had the leadership, integrity, and problem-solving practice he needed from all the consistent work he did in more obscure roles.

It's important to clarify something in Proverbs 22:29. It does not say, "Work hard and you'll become a king." It says that if you work hard, you'll be *invited to serve* kings. At the end of the day, we don't work hard and then finally graduate to a place where we are no longer serving someone. No. If we work hard, we'll be able to *serve*. Serve kings.

As Christ-followers we believe that Jesus is the ultimate King. We believe that in everything we do, we are serving Him and serving His people. Hopefully we get skilled in our field and get all the promotions and hit all of our career goals. Hopefully we do all the things! If we don't, hopefully we still use where we are as an opportunity to serve. If we do, hopefully we use it all to better serve God and serve His people. Service is not the means to the end; service is always the goal.

> Service is always the goal.

It's Not Just Work. It's Worship.

There is a reason Joseph learned from those before him, why he was invested instead of entitled, why excellence was his brand, and why he led before he was a leader. He wasn't doing it for man—not for Potiphar, Pharaoh, or the jailer. Even as Joseph was at the cusp of his greatest promotion, about to interpret Pharaoh's dream, he said in Genesis 41:16: "It is beyond my power to do this. . . . But God can tell you what it means and set you at ease" (NLT). Joseph saw all of his work as an opportunity to worship God and make Him known. Joseph gave all the glory to God when he was a slave, *and* he gave it to God in front of the king.

By the way, Joseph ended up playing a key role in saving many across close and distant lands from starvation, including his brothers who sold him, and their relationship was eventually restored. But even then, he knew that it was not by his own power that he did anything praiseworthy; it was the power of God living within him that empowered him every step of the way.

So what does this have to do with you and me revealing God's love at our day jobs?

A way for you to open the door for great relationships at your place of work is to be excellent at your work and excellent to work with. To be a compassionate coworker. To be an enthusiastic employee. To seek out and find every opportunity to serve others and serve God, even in small, unseen ways. At the very least, it will give you the opportunity to serve more. And that's always been the goal.

PARTIES, POEMS, AND PRETTY COOL FESTIVALS

Most of the friends I made at open mics and poetry slams also didn't know Jesus. The same principles applied there. I may not have been the most naturally talented, but I was going far in competitions because of how hard I worked and how prepared I was. I was packing out workshops, helping new poets write clearer and seasoned poets memorize quicker. This allowed me to be invited to more events and to create more trusted relationships. People knew I was a Jesus girl and maybe that made their eyebrows raise and guards come up at first. But over time I had respect in the field. This Jesus girl was also a competitive artist who was actively training other artists. We shared the love of storytelling. This commonality was an open door.

I shared this chapter with a handful of my peers, and one

vulnerably admitted that she doesn't feel like she knows anyone who doesn't love Jesus. Her place of work is filled with people dedicated to serving Him. How then does she share God's love to those who are far from Him, if she doesn't know people who are far from Him? It's a great question. One many might be asking.

Many people have jobs that simply don't provide a vast array of coworkers within a close vicinity. Many work in solitude or work from home, and others like my friend may only be in work environments with people who already know Jesus. If you're in any of these groups, perhaps not all of the above principles apply exactly to you.

I suppose, then, you'll need to get involved in some recreational activities that you don't actually enjoy in order to push yourself to somehow share about Jesus.

Just kidding.

What do you enjoy? What other hobbies do you have? What other social circles are you in? Remember that God wants to use who you actually are to reveal who He actually is.

Growing up in San Francisco, surrounded by artists and small-business owners, one of my great joys has always been locally made garments, jewelry, and household items. I love supporting those who have created a business, an entire artistic world, from scratch. I love when people upcycle their garments and make something worn like new. I love one-of-a-kind things. This doesn't necessarily have to do with my faith in God, but it has everything to do with what God created me to love and enjoy. And everything I am has the potential to bring Him glory and make Him known.

> God wants to use who you actually are to reveal who He actually is.

This love has led me to become a frequent customer at small boutique shops and artisan festivals. It's led me to tiny art galleries bursting with bright colors and eccentric shapes, and it's led me to small hole-in-the-wall fashion shows with funky, fringed textiles and feather-lined hats. (Don't imagine the high-end New York Fashion Week with runway models. Imagine a glorified basement with a small batch of some of the coolest and strangest clothes you've ever seen. I'll take one of each, please!) Over the years, I've developed longtime friendships with many founders and makers. Though almost none of us had religious beliefs in common, we shared a love for handmade art. This common passion bonded us. When I first started sharing Jesus through spoken poems and sermons throughout the country, I, too, began to struggle with what my friend admitted to wrestling with: *Am I mostly surrounded with people who already know Jesus?* I made sure to not abandon my love for local craftsmanship and the people it has brought me close to.

When you're considering how to form relationships with people far from God, remember what you love to do and the passions you have, then step into the spaces you love and it won't be so awkward. Unlock the power of commonality to build authentic relationships, and you will find opportunities you never imagined possible.

We are not here to trap anyone. We are not tasked to trick people. We have the answer to their soul's greatest longings. And taking the time to get to know them, their language, and their lens, with lots of listening and care, will likely need to happen before trust is established. Then it will take sharing about the freedom you have found in Jesus, the One who has changed your entire life.

The good news is that you're not selling tickets to a spiritual show they're not yet interested in. You're inviting them to a freer, more healed life that they long for but may express in different words. Jesus didn't come as a dictator. Jesus didn't come as a law enforcer. Jesus came to be a friend, to make friends, and to set all

His friends free. Jesus didn't think the world needed more high-and-mighty egocentric leadership. He thought the world could use more real friends.

Commonality is a powerful thing. It's such a powerful thing that Jesus came to have it with us, to be human like us, to experience emotions and temptations like us (Heb. 4:15), to speak truth to where we were, and set us free from everything that holds us back from a relationship with God. He stepped into our world. He calls us to do the same with others.

> Jesus came to be a friend, to make friends, and to set all His friends free.

COOKIES, CAMPFIRES, AND VICTORY

Whenever I smell freshly baked chocolate chip cookies, I think of my friends Sean and Shelley. I'm reminded of a short time of living with them and their beautiful daughters in a home filled with laughter and adventure while I was on the road. I'll share more about them in an upcoming chapter (you're going to love them), but for now, what you need to know is that Shelley is a master baker. So whenever the scent of melting chocolate and warm butter exhales from any kitchen, I close my eyes, inhale, and smile, recalling the fond memories of that time when my everyday life was a part of theirs.

Whenever I smell a campfire, I think of my husband, Guy, and me catching up with my in-laws, Bill and Sue, around a firepit on Lake Michigan. In the summer we visit them at a lake house that they built from the ground up. We catch up about the highs and lows of the year, the best films we've seen, the weirdest things happening at work, and the craziest things all our friends did that year. We eat way too many chips and all the dips, Guy and Bill barbecue the best meats, and Sue and I laugh our heads off at ourselves. We think we're pretty hilarious and need no additional entertainment. It's a simple time, rich in the company and the joy of being present in the moment, together.

Chocolate chip cookies and campfires may not bring the same supersized smile to your face that they bring to mine, but my guess is that you have smells that take you back to wonderfully nostalgic places, other dimensions filled with scenes from your life that you love to replay. A certain flower. A specific food. A particular perfume. It's difficult to describe a scent. You can't see it. I can't draw you the smell of a campfire or provide nearly enough adjectives that give the holy aroma of fresh cookies its full justice.

What's my point? Jesus people are called to be a sweet aroma to everyone around them—a scent of life, a fragrance of possibilities, a "sense of joy" (2 Cor. 5:12). It may shock us to discover that unveiling the love of Jesus is rarely a speech we have folded in our pockets for anytime someone asks us about our faith. It's more like the aroma of chocolate chip cookies bubbling over with godly things like butter and the excitement of enjoying this with someone you love spending time with, the savory smells alone providing you a sense of joy, a calmer spirit, and a better day.

Paul wrote in 2 Corinthians that God "leads us in Christ's triumphal procession and through us spreads the aroma of the knowledge of him in every place. For to God we are the fragrance of Christ among those who are being saved and among those who are perishing" (2:14–15 csb).

Paul's letters were written at a time when triumphant parades were a part of the culture. (Wouldn't it be awesome to bring that back? I'm all in for my husband and all my friends dancing around my house and singing whenever I hit a deadline. We'll see if they go for it. I'll shoot my shot.) The Roman Empire had a tradition that when soldiers returned home from a victorious battle, they'd march through the streets in celebration, flags raised high, generals waving at the front, locals coming out of their homes to cheer and chant. And the aroma of a specific incense reserved for the occurrence of victory would commandeer the air.

Even if people couldn't yet hear it or see it, they would smell the evidence. This aroma told the town there had been a triumph. Something inside of them was reminded of victory. Likewise, Paul was saying to the church, "Your life is evidence to people that victory is here. Even before they hear it proclaimed, something in them senses the presence of life, joy, and freedom."

When people feel defeated, they are attracted to the scent of victory. Jesus people should be a breath of fresh air in a toxic, suffocating world.

What is the scent of your life?

You may say, "Bath & Body Works Cucumber Melon body lotion and Old Spice Pure Sport deodorant!" Not exactly what we're talking about, but it probably wouldn't hurt pointing people to Jesus by smelling good.

What is the X factor surrounding your life that brings people a sense of joy, peace, and excitement about their own life? When you are truly filled by God's power and have the Holy Spirit living within you, you produce a loving life demonstrating joy in hard times, peace in chaos, enduring patience, active kindness, virtuous decisions, unwavering faith, compassionate gentleness, and a spirit strengthened with self-control (Gal. 5:22–23).

- When other teachers at the school you work at are being rude and irritable toward one another, you can have a consistent spirit of kindness, patience, and problem-solving.
- When other baristas at the coffee shop you work at are being negative about one another and the environment feels suffocating, you can go out of your way to breathe out some fresh, calming air, creating an environment of encouragement.
- When your coworkers are crude, gossiping, and being divisive, you can go out of your way to stand up for and include those that others leave out and raise the standard of how people speak to one another in your workplace. You can be gentle and peaceful and be a new example others start to follow.

When I smell our neighborhood's basketball gym, reeking of sweat and old sneakers, I have to wrinkle my nose in preparation for going in. I love the game of basketball, but the smell of active gyms and packed locker rooms is certainly a price to be paid.

We can just as easily be a scent that does not smell of anything good at all. We can make people never want to be around us because we're constantly complaining, or we can make them try to avoid us because we're always making fun of someone else. Without realizing it, we can become a gag-provoking odor that pushes people away with arrogance, pride, and a lack of compassion.

- We can push people away by the graceless, aggressive way we speak to people we don't agree with on social media.
- We can push people away by the shame we give people who aren't living up to our own standards or moral codes.
- We can push people away when we fight to be right over fighting for a relationship.

Like a point guard, I'm calling it: the way we treat people often speaks louder than the words we say to them.

What do your actions say to those right next to you? More than the words that come out of you, what is it like to be around you?

When we treat people in ways that reflect how Jesus treated people, those around us should see the physical evidence of how welcoming and loving Jesus is. People will be drawn to that. People will be drawn to Him. Nobody hates being loved.

> The way we treat people often speaks louder than the words we say to them.

AN EXPERT AT FUMBLING

It's taken me some time to learn how to reveal God's love through intentional relationships, and it's taken me years to learn how to naturally talk about Jesus. Once I started, I learned what made people feel small and offended and what made people feel respected and empowered. I learned what made people feel pushed away and isolated and what made people feel invited and connected. Fumbling through it has been my greatest teacher. The more I talked about Jesus, the better I got at talking about Jesus.

Showing people the love of Jesus is worth fumbling a couple of times. And worth saying the wrong words sometimes. Remember, the hardest part is already finished. Sins are forgiven. Death is conquered. Once we choose Jesus, our future is guaranteed to have full healing and eternal life. We can't ruin that. Instead, we've been entrusted by God to reveal His love to the people right next to us. Whenever you start to ask yourself, *How do I love people well? What is the right formula? What are the exact right words?* here is a step: Care more about the people you are talking to than the words that you are saying to them. Love people more than you love the words you're saying. When you do, you will start to speak with real love, show real love, and when we all do that, we will be surrounded by people who know how loved they are. We can be a part of creating that kind of world.

Don't try to be anybody else. Be more of who you are. Through your common workplace and common interests, invest in people's lives, share the truth about your life, serve people, show up for people, really love people more than your own words, and bring a real sense of joy into your relationships. Not just as a means to an end but because Jesus loves it when we're good friends. He loves it when we spend time with people, eating meals and sharing stories. That's how He chose to spend His days on earth too.

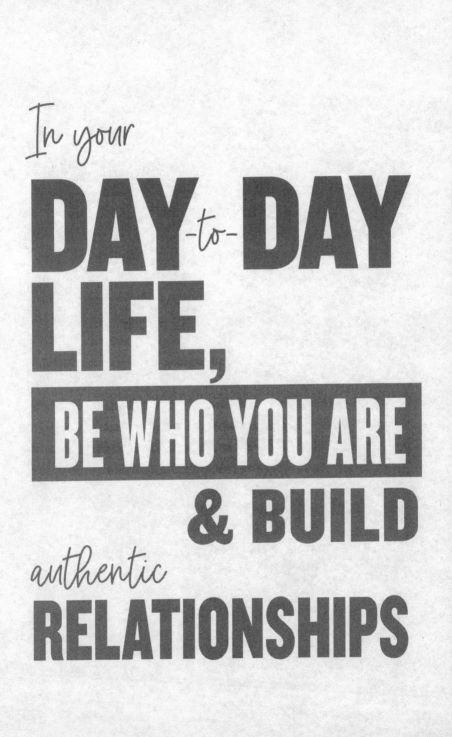

In your **DAY**-to-**DAY LIFE,** BE WHO YOU ARE & BUILD *authentic* RELATIONSHIPS

How (not) to Save the World

#8 | Live to Please People

My mom began her second act at the age of fifty-five. Faithful and fruitful in continuing the ministry she forged with my dad in the late '80s, under my mom's leadership, our family's outreach provided food for hundreds of families and saw many who were once in despair and addiction surrender their vices and start a relationship with Jesus. Even though my dad had passed, his work continued.

Though my leadership grew in the ministry over the years, and I led aspects of it remotely, my mom stepped up and became the hardcore, on-the-ground, hands-on leader. She lovingly led our volunteer teams, grew our relationships with the San Francisco–Marin Food Bank and the surrounding ballparks,[a] opened our ministry's first

---

a. Our outreach got hundreds of leftover ballpark hot dogs and burgers from the San Francisco 49ers' and Giants' stadiums after their games, and we'd reheat them for our service the next day. Whenever it was game day, our friends on the streets would say, "Oowee, I know what tomorrow's lunch is!" That's right, we were the *cool* ministry! The hot-dog people! Let's go Niners! Let's go Giants! Let's go ketchup!

weekly food pantry, and in my dad's absence, organized a rotation of many other pastors and worship leaders in the Bay Area who came to preach and lead at our services each week. Much to her surprise, when *she* preached for the first time, hesitantly inserting herself into the roster, something in the downtown air shifted.

At this point we were holding our services in a spacious, echoey recreation room in the middle of the Tenderloin district, as opposed to our early years in a park. Whenever my mom spoke, our friends living on the streets would come from around the block to hear and support the preacher's wife. Even if the room was too full, their ears would press against the cold glass windows, their eyes peeking through the cracked-open doors. She had more authority on those streets than she knew.

The day came when my mom wondered if leading this ministry was still what God was calling her to do or if she was spending her days living out my dad's calling. It was a hard question to say out loud. Though brave, the words tasted bitter. He was her world and so was his mission. Their work together was important. There was no easy way to navigate this seed of an unexpected feeling now growing within her. She wrestled with what it would mean to have less of a role in our outreach and to instead pursue something else entirely.

I asked her, "What do you want to do?"

Instead of answering what she wanted to do, she answered with all the reasons why she could not possibly do anything else.

"I think my time to start over has passed."

"I'm too old."

"I only have a high school diploma."

"No one starts a career at my age."

"If I go to school for anything, all the other students will be younger. I will stick out."

"Maybe I'm being selfish. My life is fine as it is."

For months I tried to hear through her fears and interpret her introspection, investigating what was stirring in her heart to venture out toward. Finally, across the kitchen table in my childhood home, a tattered blue-and-white-checkered tablecloth with sunflowers lining the edges under our elbows, I leaned in. The old cloth, which for years had needed to be replaced, ripped the slightest bit beneath my arms. "Mom. Stop thinking about all the reasons you can't. Just tell me. What is the biggest, craziest, out-of-this-world dream you have?"

She stared at me, eyes wide, almost guilty, clenching her hands, raising her shoulders, and releasing her answer as if breathing out a sigh of relief: "I want to be a preschool teacher."

Her body relaxed. She was as shocked at her answer as I was.

Our gazes held.

Finally, I broke our silent staring contest. Reaching my hand across the table to grab her now relaxed hands, I said, "Okay, Mom. Let's make it happen."

My mom did not have any one specific person telling her she could not step into what she was feeling pulled in her heart to do. Instead, she was discouraged by an imaginary status quo and expected timeline she felt she was missing, her fears of what people would say, and how it would look to try to do something new in this season of her life.

Whether visible or not, all of us have fallen victim to this sudden freezing—a pause in our purpose due to people's expectations.

Throughout my life I commonly felt that I was too young to do the things I believed God was calling me to do. Much like the height requirement before getting on a roller coaster—I was just a little too short. My mom was in a season where she now felt she was too old, exceeding the requirements to get back on the ride. Who made these requirements? When it comes to obeying God, who built this tall yellow measuring stick in the middle of this loud theme park called life that we look at to see, "Are you the right height? Are you the right age? Do you have the qualifications deemed worthy?"

We have all felt at times like we are missing the mark.

- We don't have the exact amount of resources we need.
- We don't have the perfect team we want.
- We don't have the most experience.
- We have too much experience.
- We would be the only woman.
- We would be the only man.
- We would be the youngest.
- We would be the oldest.
- No one else is doing this.
- Everybody else is doing this.

Whose measuring stick are we trying to live up to? It certainly is not God's.

We have not only disqualified ourselves from positions or roles based on other people's standards, opinions, or seeming expectations but also disqualified our *stories*, and we've held in what God has done in our lives.

- My story is not as good as other people's stories.
- My life is too different.
- My life is not different enough.
- My life is too broken.
- My life is not broken enough.
- No one else has a story like me.
- Everyone else has a story like me.

How can we live for Jesus and show the world Jesus if we are always trying to please the world Jesus came to save?

I am more certain of this today than ever: Living to please people? That's how (not) to save the world. If we believe that *people* hold our ultimate value, then we settle on their human standards, missing out on the God-sized mission of showing people how valuable *they* are.

As I've shared, I've lived obsessed with other people's opinions throughout many seasons of my life. Worried that I didn't have the right background, I wasn't the right gender, I wasn't the right race, and I didn't have the right story, I've held back my obedience and have many times lived to please man instead of God. There were times I spent all of my time and energy on the tops of my tippy-toes reaching toward their expectations. At times, I did reach them. Go me! I achieved the success I longed for! I received the applause I lived for! Then the status quo changed. The world's judges had new criteria in place, and success was redefined. Let me tell you, living to please the world is an exhausting, never-ending race where the rules are ever-changing, the finish line keeps moving, and the awards don't last. Living to please the world is simply unfulfilling.

I want to echo the words of Paul, who asked, "Do you think I am trying to please people? If I were doing that, I would not be a servant of Christ" (Gal. 1:10 CEV). We cannot accomplish both pleasing the world and pleasing God. If we are slaves to what people are saying, then we can't be obedient to what God is saying. We cannot take the step of faith God is calling us to take while making everybody else happy with our every move.

If you live to please people, and not to please God, you will never step into the full purpose God has for your life. You will never write the songs God has called you to write because you are afraid they are *too different* or *too similar* to the other ones you have heard. Then the songs God has put in you will never be heard, and people will not be brought closer to the presence of God through the words He has put in you. You will never start the small group at your house you feel called to start because you don't think you know the Bible as well as other small group leaders. Then the students in your neighborhood will not be discipled by someone they know and trust. You will never share the gospel through spoken-word poetry around the country. You will never become a preschool teacher in your fifties. People will not know Jesus if we keep living to please the people Jesus came to save.

> **People will not know Jesus if we keep living to please the people Jesus came to save.**

MRS. WONG'S CLASS

My mom's hand shook as she turned the rusty knob and opened the off-white door to her community-college classroom, the uneven blinds bouncing off the door's window as she took her first step into getting her teaching credentials. Seeing a room filled with students half her age, she was more terrified than she had been in decades, but she opened the door and took her seat. She gasped a few weeks later when she got back her first test, a ginormous, bright red A+ painted at the top of the page. Raindrops of joy trickled down her cheeks as she completed her first semester, then her second, then her third. She grinned from ear to ear after her first day at work as a teacher at a Christian preschool. Skipping to her car on her way to drive home, she FaceTimed me and exclaimed, "I love my students! This is my dream job!"

She did it.

My mom has now been a preschool teacher for a couple of years. Living in this new era of her life, she told me, "This is what I'm supposed to be doing. I know this is where I'm supposed to be."

My friend, forget the status quo. Tear up the invisible timeline you have referenced for what you are supposed to do and when you are supposed to do it. You are rarely too old or too young. It is rarely too late or too early. Your calling is rarely parallel to the other people in your community, in your church, or in your life phase. Take the limits off of yourself. Take the limits off of God. God is calling each and every single one of us, but He is not calling us to the same things. What a loss it would be to live by the standards and timelines of man as opposed to the call of God. What a tragedy it would be to wish we were in a different life phase so much so that we miss the important one we are in now.

There is something different God wants to do in us and through us in every season of our lives. Don't rush it. Don't skip it. Bring the fullness of who you are and all that is inside of you to the moment you are actually living in. In this moment you're living right now, God has something specific for you to grab hold of and something specific for you to give.

We must not forget the words of Paul, which remind us of the sacred process God wants to journey with us. He said, "There has never been the slightest doubt in my mind that the God who started this great work in you would keep at it and bring it to a flourishing finish on the very day Christ Jesus appears" (Phil. 1:6 MSG).

The lie: to be used by God your life needs to look a certain way at a certain time and meet a particular earthly standard.

The truth: God handmade you a certain way and placed you in a particular time to be used in ways you cannot predict or comprehend. His timelines are better than the world's timelines. His plans are better than our plans. When we live to please God, He is able to use every detail of our lives and every step of obedience to complete the work He wants to do in us and through us.

HIDING HOPE

Sometimes the people we are living to impress are the same people God has put in our lives for us to impact.

When I started performing spoken-word poetry in secular venues, my initial instinct was to only share pieces that left Jesus out and try to keep my faith a secret for as long as I could. I had a good reason—I wanted to make friends in these arenas! I was afraid that if I shouted about Jesus at the top of my lungs every second, pushed my church onto everybody in every conversation, and judged and condemned my fellow artists every day, they would not want to be friends with me.

I was right.

If I did any of *those things,* they would absolutely *not* be friends with me. I also would not want to be friends with that kind of person. That person sounds awful to be around! It turned out, there was a way to share about who I really am, and my real story, and learn about *them*, and *their* real story, without being uninviting or aggressive. I had to discover that way.

In the New Testament we learn of many religious leaders who did not believe Jesus was who He said He was, but we rarely talk of the leaders who *did* believe He was the Savior and yet held in their faith in fear of man.

John told us that "many rulers believed in Jesus. However, they wouldn't admit it publicly because the Pharisees would have thrown them out of the synagogue. They were more concerned about what people thought of them than about what God thought of them" (John 12:42–43 GW). These leaders believed in Jesus but did not want to say that out loud for fear of other people's disapproval. But if Jesus was the Savior, *actually* the Savior . . . no, really, if He was the real-life Breaker of Chains, Healer of Hearts, and Freer of Addictions, why would they keep it from the very people He came to set free? They accepted Jesus as the Savior, but they didn't want Him to actually save?

I did not want to hold back the truth of a wonderful Rescuer from my newfound friends because I feared they would not like me. Jesus loves my friends like crazy and had uniquely positioned me in this underground slam-poetry world. I was right to think that being pushy and aggressive was not the best way to show them Jesus. I was wrong that being silent and hiding the hope of Jesus inside of myself was the best thing for my friends. I was wrong that they didn't want joy and peace. I was wrong that they did not want to live out their full purpose. I was wrong that being accepted by man was more important than my friends knowing they were accepted by God. As I mentioned in the last chapter, over time, I learned to talk about Him naturally.

- He was in the poems I shared onstage. "I'm not who I used to be. Someone changed me. Something changed inside of me . . ."
- He was in my schedule and calendar. "Yes, I can come to dinner after church, we are having this awesome food drive after our service, but I'll come out after. Can't wait!"
- He was in my invitations. "Do you want to come to church and the food drive with me? There are other artists there I'd love you to meet. Then we'll meet up with everyone after. I can drive us."
- He was in my conversations. "I'm so sorry you lost that opportunity. My heart hurts with you. You already know I'm going to pray for you. I'm going to pray God opens more doors. Better

doors. Bigger doors." (PS: No one has ever told me, "Please don't pray that God opens doors for me.")

- He was in my story. "I can relate to not feeling enough. I've lived a lot of my life feeling like I'm not making the mark either. Like I shared in my spoken-word piece, I meant it, learning about a God who loved me anyway and finding my confidence in Him changed my life. I know the season you're in is so hard, and I can't imagine all you're feeling. I just want you to know I'm here; I'm with you; you're not alone."

Being myself and being honest are far better ways to make friends, keep friends, and show my friends Jesus.

I used to think there were two options:

1. Share your faith as aggressively as possible, spout impressive theological monologues, and if people don't accept the truth you're saying, Oh well! Their loss! At least you were obedient! Box: checked.
2. Keep the Person who set you free and changed your life hidden. Don't talk about Jesus; don't talk about the details of your actual story; instead, stay incognito and accepted by those who don't yet know God.

The bad news is that neither of those methods points people to the One who can heal their hearts and change their lives. Neither of those options show the people you love how loved they are.

It takes consistent, authentic, loving relationships where you are, with the people around you, to reveal God's love. It's less monologues and more dialogues. It's less excluding and more engaging. It's more checking yes on RSVPs than no. It's lots of various, random, specific-to-you-and-your-friends things. But it's never yelling. It's also never ignoring. It's neither being pushy nor being absent. It's neither being obnoxiously loud nor fearfully silent. It's presence and truth. It's authentic with-ness. It's an aroma of victory. It's a sense of joy. You can speak naturally about Jesus by giving welcoming invitations, having honest conversations, and sharing your real story.

Some people may still not receive your invitations. That's okay. Live in the freedom of being who you are to the people God has placed right in front of you, and trust that you are not fighting for your friends alone. God is working alongside of you and wants to partner with you in showing your friends who He is. Some

> You can speak naturally about Jesus by giving welcoming invitations, having honest conversations, and sharing your real story.

people may live up to your fears and have harsh words about your faith. Other Christ-followers may have left a bad taste in their mouth, and your friends may not be excited to have another Jesus-person around. That's okay too. You can show them what a person who really loves Jesus and really loves people is like. It may be your relationship with them that helps them see how loved and valuable they truly are.

IT'S EXACTLY YOU

God wants to use exactly who you are in this moment to reach those far from Him today. Don't aim to become like anyone else. Don't aim to please anyone else. Whether you are single or married, someone with no kids or eighteen kids, someone with all the resources or with none, someone with a giant sphere of influence or nothing more than a cheap microphone at your local coffee shop's open mic with four people in the audience,[b] there is something about your specific season that is important for the work God wants to do in and through you. Your story is the story He wants you to share. Your gifts are the gifts He wants you to have. Your community is the community He wants you to reach. Your age and your life phase are what He wants to use to do something awesome for you and for others around you.

> There is something about your specific season that is important for the work God wants to do in and through you.

Thank goodness there's something bigger happening, exceeding our timelines, expectations, and presuppositions. Thank goodness there's a Designer who has made us on purpose and placed us on purpose. Thank goodness there's a way for the people in our lives to know Jesus. It's exactly us. It's exactly me. It's exactly you.

If you only live to please people, follow culture's timelines and preferences, and hide who you are and the hope you have for fear of rejection, you will miss out on what Jesus wants to do in and through your life. And so will your friends. Instead, throw the man-made measuring stick out the window. Burn the playbook. Don't live chained to pleasing people. Live to partner with God in setting people free.

Your season may not be the same as my season or their season.

---

b. When I was eighteen, a spoken-word piece I wrote catapulted my platform in the secular slam-poetry scene. It was the most honest and raw piece I had written at the time, and I had no idea how it would relate to people. It opened doors for me I never imagined and put me on a journey of being surrounded and trained by some of the most well-known underground slam poets at the time. I attribute a lot of my knowledge of competitive slam poetry and oral storytelling to the lessons I learned from that piece at eighteen years of age. The first time I performed it was at a small coffee shop's open mic with a microphone that barely worked and four people in the audience. Three were my friends. And one was the owner of another venue who invited me to come to his open mic next.

And it's not supposed to be. God wants to make sure that every gap is filled and every need is met. Every role is important. Every season matters. Be who you really are and say yes to what God is calling you to do in this season right now. Why? Because we need poets at open mics, coaches at basketball games, single moms starting small groups for single moms, entrepreneurs mentoring young business minds, preachers in parks serving the streets for twenty years, and fifty-five-year-olds teaching preschool for the first time. That's how God's love will be made known to every person everywhere.

Instead of living **chained to PLEASING PEOPLE,** Live to **PARTNER with GOD IN SETTING PEOPLE** Free

How (not) to Save the World

#9 | Compare Yourself to Others

I'll never forget the coolest outfit I ever wore. Junior high was when kids were learning how to care for their shining constellations of acne, be kinder to the cutie they were crushing on, and most important, rock the cool brands. Someone would walk into class with a flashy new shirt, large logo spread across the front, and I'd watch as my classmates would be in awe of it. *How do they even know what that is? Where do you go to learn what is cool?* If I told my dad I was growing out of my current clothes, he'd give me ten dollars and wait in the car as I tried to collect all that I could at our neighborhood's thrift store. I had to get creative, create my own style, and eventually learn the basics of sewing to make the limited items available fit me correctly. But I didn't want kids at school to know that. Captivated by my classmates with greater means and larger groups of friends, I spent my young teen years obsessed with what they wore, what they listened to, and what they deemed "in." I tried to keep up. I *had* to figure out what the cool brands were.

The day came when a new store opened in my neighborhood. My neighbors talked about how this store was usually in nicer areas than ours and would probably bring with it a slew of more upscale stores. I decided whatever store it was, I was going to get an outfit from there. And when it came, I certainly did.

The store was Jamba Juice.

The smoothie-selling sensation was dancing its way into our taste buds and shopping centers (and into our hearts), and I was determined to wear items from this clearly trendy and hip store. (Never mind that it wasn't actually a clothing store—that was a small detail—they had merch!) A girl from our church worked there and hooked me up with a baby-blue Jamba Juice T-shirt, a matching Jamba Juice hat (I figured, *Cool people match, right?*), a Jamba Juice tote bag, a Jamba Juice football (painted in the same colors as the Jamba swirl, obviously, *this is fashion*), and myriad Jamba Juice promotional pins I scattered among the hat, shirt, and tote. I confidently wore all of these items together to school the next day.

I like to think of myself as the original Instagram influencer. Jamba Juice hasn't paid me yet, but I'm sure that check is coming. (Dear Jamba, holla at your girl!) I wore that outfit once a week for over a month and a half, until one day my dad said to me, "Hosanna, is it Career Day again?"

Boooooo.

I knew it was time to retire the jersey, put the outfit away, and resort once again to my hemmed-up secondhand finds.

Comparison is a horrible thing. And frankly, it's exhausting. As kids, it causes us to think more about what other kids have than what we have, rank ourselves among each other, and gossip about those we deem better than or less than us. It causes us to bully, out of superiority or insecurity, just so others know what our personal ranks are, and it makes some of us obsessed with trying to impress everyone else (though we have no proof my classmates *weren't* impressed by my smoothie-store merchandise and matching football).

As we get older, *sure*, we grow more confident in our external tastes being different from that of our friends and our lifestyles being in our own lane, but we certainly don't grow out of the evils of comparing ourselves to others altogether. For many of us, our adolescent years are faint in contrast to the ways that comparison rears its ugly head later in life.

- You see that other woman online who has a calling that's similar to yours—she's also a writer and mentor to young girls—but she has more resources and better graphics on social media. How can you look just a little more like her? Or a little better than her? You spend more time obsessing over *her* newest, next thing than praying and thinking on what God is calling *you* to do next.

- You know the dad across the street is also a coach—but he's coaching more teams, hosting more team get-togethers, and bringing more kids to church events than you. You ask your wife, "What am I doing wrong?" constantly calculating his seeming success versus yours. You complain about how loud his outdoor barbecue parties are and start making snide comments, spending more time tearing him down than building him up and bonding over your shared goal.

- You notice the worship leader who is also serving their local church or see that photographer who also has a successful blog. You research to see the number of followers they have online and compare their number of likes and comments to yours.

- You hear that spoken-word artist you *just know* you can perform better than, see that graphic designer you know you can design better than, meet that leader you're sure you can lead better than, and constantly measure your résumé and reputation against theirs. It consumes your time, thoughts, energy, and conversations.

We often compare ourselves to someone who is a *lot* like us, just one step ahead or behind. And it brings out the worst in us. Comparison causes us to root for those behind us but not those who have surpassed us. As long as they stay behind us, we're a fan. As their achievements seem to grow past ours, our cheers grow silent. This shows that we are not cheering for what God *is doing* in others; we are cheering for what we *like* God doing in others. Sometimes we see people with callings so similar to ours and begin to believe the lie that there must not be room for both of us. God must have called too many people to the field we're called to. Who will win out this coveted space in the end? We're ready to either put our fists up and fight for it or throw our hands in the air and give up.

I wish I had learned this earlier in my life. Comparing yourself to others? That's how (not) to save the world. If God has called all of us, there's not just room for all of us, there's a need for all of us. If you step back from the call of God on your life, the Enemy wins. If the person you're comparing yourself to steps back from the call of God on their life, the Enemy wins. If we all succeed in taking our competition down, the Enemy wins the most. If you fight against what God has called someone to do, you are fighting against God.

> **If you fight against what God has called someone to do, you are fighting against God.**

Followers of Jesus are not your competition; they are your coworkers. God needs all of us to accomplish His work. The best-case scenario is that we all succeed in what God has called us to do and we all work together to accomplish God's mission. The cheering section should be where we live.

REBUILD AND REPAIR

After more than 140 years of the Jews living in captivity, exile, and ruins, Nehemiah cast a vision to rebuild the walls of the broken-down city of Jerusalem. The city was shattered—crumbled stone scattered for miles, cockroaches scurrying around, skeletons of people and dogs piled along unpaved roads, and dirty footprints stamped on walls that once stood tall but had been knocked down by the opposing armies. The task at hand was far too great for one person to accomplish. This was not going to be like a group project in school where one overachieving student finishes the whole thing.[a] Nehemiah cast a vision for a better strategy. In order to carry the mission out, "the priests made repairs, each in front of his own house" (Neh. 3:28 NIV).

To accomplish the great task at hand, each person had to assess the situation right in front of them and use the tools they had right in front of them in order to rebuild what was right in front of them.

We will not rebuild our cities and restore our communities if we're comparing what is in front of us to what is in front of someone else. Critiquing how someone else is building, instead of looking at what God has given us to build, is the surefire way to guarantee that nothing gets built at all. The Enemy hopes we're too distracted by what other people have and what other people are doing to discover the

---

a. Some of you may be thinking, *I loved those projects; I never did a thing!* And as the one Chinese kid in my class growing up who did everyone's projects, you're welcome.

beauty and power of who we are, what we have, and what God has called us to do.

Don't waste one second of your precious life comparing yourself to the other people God has also called to His mission. Instead, ask yourself what God has put in front of you.

By my count in the King James Version, the Hebrew word *bānâ*, translated as *build* or *rebuild*, occurs seven times in Nehemiah 3, and the Hebrew term *hāzaq*, translated as *repair*, occurs thirty-five times. In some places the city's walls and buildings were a tragic mess with no structure. They needed to be reimagined, planned out, and built from the ground up. In other places, some structures were merely unfinished, cracked, or out of order, with repairs needing to be made to the existing structures.

When you look around your community, your home, and your relationships and assess the situation, what's right in front of you? In what way can you be a part of a solution? Is it something that needs to be built from the ground up—something that doesn't yet exist? Or is it a repair that needs to be made to an existing system? Both are needed.

- Is there a program to help tutor students that your city needs but doesn't yet have? Does something need to be started, built from the ground up?
- Is there a relationship in your family that you need to reconcile? Something you did that you need to apologize for? Someone you need to forgive? Does something right in front of you need to be repaired?
- In your place of work, in your field, at your church, in your school, you know what your coworkers and classmates are going through, and you have a specific perspective of what people in your community need. What is something brand new that you

could start in order to bless and build up those around you? What is a way that your words or your actions could repair something that's been shattered?

God is asking each of us to be aware of the need right in front of us and faithful with the task He has put before us.

When it comes to other people doing the best they can to use the gifts they have, striving to be obedient and live out their purpose—we *can't* compete with that; that's God's handiwork. Working against God's people is working against God. Don't compare yourself to other builders. It will take all of us to rebuild and repair.

ANGELS, SUNSETS, AND OREO CAKES

Earlier today I left my New York hotel room to take a walk around Manhattan before a dinner meeting. Crossing bustling streets lined with golden taxi cabs and determined joggers, I was captivated by the sun sinking behind the mixed bag of majestic skyscrapers propped up by bodegas and hole-in-the-wall pizza joints. Together, the varied sizes and statures of brick and stone structures created an array of opportunities for the light to break through. The lemon hues of the bright sun were warming up into apricot tones, a nostalgic invitation beckoning locals and tourists alike.

"Excuse me, can I get some money?"

I turned to notice a man approaching me from the side. He was dripping with sweat, no doubt due to him wearing heavy cotton sweatpants and a sweatshirt on a humid, ninety-degree day in Manhattan. His odor told me that it had been days or weeks since his last shower. I did not have cash, I explained to him, so I took him to a nearby deli

I'd noticed a few blocks away where I could buy him a meal with my credit card. His name was Angel, and he shared a bit of his story as we walked the glistening streets in mid-sunset.

Angel spoke of the New Jersey neighborhood he was raised in, his past seven years living in New York, and the pains of his current condition. He was without a job, without a home, and hungry. He asked me for an orange soda and said he needed a bar of soap—a modest request that I was happy to grant. But once we arrived at the deli, the request turned into a full-blown shopping palooza. I was far from annoyed. I'll never forget how happy he was that the deli had Oreo chocolate cake and how disappointed he was that they didn't sell scissors for him to cut his sweatpants into shorts. This short trip to the store mattered to him.

As we left the deli, with a crate of Angel's new groceries and belongings, I asked him if I could pray for him. He was immediately evasive, mentioning that he'd love prayer but was scared of God. I let him know I used to feel that way, too, until I learned that our Creator is more loving than we've sometimes been led to believe and that He's always ready to talk to us, heal us, and make us whole whenever we want to invite Him in. His eyes widened. I assured him that guilt and shame weren't exactly God's thing, and I was sorry that he had been told that.

His demeanor changed and his shoulders relaxed as he allowed me to pray over him. But Angel was taken aback when I then asked him to pray for me.

It was clear as he spoke to God about me that he had prayed before. He used phrases like "Father God" and asked God to "bless this sister like she has blessed me." Those words told me he had spoken to our Father before and had probably done at least a short stint in church at some point.

His prayer went longer than mine, and after he said, "Amen," I reminded Angel that God is always available, and if he wanted to give his life to Him today, I could help him do that. Staring at the concrete he replied, "No, I'm not ready yet." I told him that I'd be praying for him, today was fun, and it was awesome to meet him. He looked up, thanked me, and then he was gone.

As I headed back toward my hotel, I could not shake the guilty pit in my stomach and the plaguing thought replaying in my mind. *I should have done more.*

My childhood need to be a savior and rely on my own power reared its ugly head once again, and I began to spiral in my hurricane of should-haves.

Perhaps you can relate. You've invited coworkers to come to an event, and they've declined the offer, and you've thought, *I should have asked better.* You've posted a blog online, hoping many would read your testimony, but after a few comments were left, you thought, *I should have phrased this better.* You've planned an event and expected hundreds to show up, and as forty-two people sat scattered among folding chairs, the vacancy of the room too obvious to bear, you thought, *I know so many other people who would have planned this better. Why did I even attempt this?* Like my encounter with Angel, we spin in circles of all the people who perhaps could have pulled off what we didn't.

NOT THE POINT(S)

As I headed toward my work meeting on that East Coast evening, the sun having set and the breeze from the Hudson River coming in to greet me, I couldn't help but think how my dad would have spoken to Angel better. My dad would have known the right words to say. *If my dad were here, Angel and his whole family would have been in church by now, signing up for a small group and recording a testimony video.*

I had watched my dad preach the gospel to men just like Angel so passionately that even on a chilly San Francisco morning, with the Bay's pearl canopy of fog above us, sweat would break from the top of his head. I watched him weep as he led many who were far from God to the feet of Jesus, some that he used to deal drugs with years ago. I can still hear the sounds of shattering fragments of glass as people would throw down their heroin needles before raising their hands in surrender. I watched as my dad led our ministry team with integrity and compassion. Many on our team were people who first found Jesus through our outreach, got clean and sober, got homes and jobs, and turned their lives completely around.

As a kid, I saw my dad as a superhero. So perhaps it was inevitable, seeing someone lead people to Jesus so spectacularly, that I would live with the self-imposed responsibility to do the same and eventually grow dizzy in a downward guilt spiral whenever I failed to live up to the example I had seen.

Fast-forward to earlier today.

I had to stop my spiraling thoughts of comparison.

When we feel like we can never do enough, we are tempted to do nothing. When we spend too much time singing our should've-could've pity anthems, we talk ourselves out of stepping out to serve others at all. When we put too much pressure on always seeing the obvious results of complete life change, we can begin to neglect the small ways God is asking us to say yes.

And yet where did we get the notion that we have to know exactly why God puts certain people in our paths? When did we start to look down on the opportunities right in front of us, in our places of work, in our spheres of influence, in front of our houses? When did our need for tangible results become the primary reason we obey God's commandment of love?

The results are not up to us. Jesus loves the people we come across more than we can ever love them. We just need to show up. We just need to be obedient. It's not about what we can do but what God can do through us when we step out in faith.

> It's not about what we can do but what God can do through us when we step out in faith.

Our struggles are not new. The early church didn't always get this right either. While some of them were giving credit to Paul for their spiritual growth and others to another church leader, Apollos, as if points were to be tallied, Paul corrected them, saying, "We each carried out our servant assignment. I planted the seed, Apollos watered the plants, but *God* made you grow. It's not the one who plants or the one who waters who is at the center of this process but God, who makes things grow" (1 Cor. 3:6–7 MSG).

None of us get credit for life change but God. We can stop our tallying. We can quit our measuring. Our scores are tied at zero: none of us are saviors. We're all partnering together to point people toward the one and only real Savior who heals and restores lives.

FAILED

Alongside my dad, I've helped feed tens of thousands of people and been a part of hundreds of men, women, and children living on the streets coming to Jesus and changing their lives around.

All by myself, my stats aren't as good.

Alone, I have bought food for and spoken at length to maybe about sixty individual men or women without homes throughout the country. That's a dozen deli sandwiches, a handful of runs to a local Walgreens for sodas, chips, Pop-Tarts, and socks, and a couple of burgers and fries shared on street corners. Out of all of those people, shared meals, and unexpected encounters on city streets I was passing through, how many have I led in a *sincere prayer* to give their life to Jesus?

Three. Two men. One woman.

Three out of sixty? By all accounts this is not an impressive success rate. If I am to be graded on my ability to "save" the strangers I meet on the city streets, then I have an enormous red-Sharpie F. (And as an overachieving Asian woman, it hurts me to even write that. This will be my first official F ever, and it stings.) It could be easy to see myself as a failure.

However, if I am to be graded on faithfulness? I'm aiming for that A.

I rarely say the perfect things, but I am committed to show up. And hey! Maybe I've planted a seed. Maybe I've watered it. Maybe three out of sixty times I've even harvested it. Most of the time, I have no idea.

I won't allow a fear of failing stop me from taking risks. I won't allow comparison to stop me from continuously serving with what I have. I won't allow pride to stop me from saying yes to the small ways I can serve others that no one may ever see.

Jesus once miraculously fed over five thousand people (with only a little boy's lunch that He multiplied . . . *so boss*) because He saw they all were hungry. And yet no conversions were recorded that day. What was the point? What *did* happen? People were fed, and Jesus' power was shown. If that's important to Jesus, that's important to me. I want to always be available to be a part of that kind of miracle.

By getting closer to the real Savior, asking for my heart to beat for what His heart beats for, and continuously seeking out people along my life's path whom I can show compassion to, I start seeing the world a little more like Jesus. I begin to rely on Him and His power a whole lot more. And I've become continuously more aware of the ways I can show people His love.

The Enemy wins, people stay in ruins, and cities remain unbuilt and unrepaired if you

- believe providing for people without converting them is pointless,
- live in constant fear of a God who you think is more concerned about your results than your obedience, or
- allow yourself to be so overwhelmed by the brokenness you read about that you do nothing at all because nothing feels significant enough.

Paul again debunked the lie that it mattered who led who to Jesus and who got the credit. He clarified, "*It doesn't matter* whether it was I or the other witnesses *who brought you the message*. What matters is that we keep preaching and that you have faith in this message" (1 Cor. 15:11).

It doesn't matter who spoke the message. It matters who heard it and who believed. It doesn't matter who gets the credit. People aren't points on a scoreboard. God isn't a college-team recruiter comparing your stats to someone else's. What matters is not the tally of results. What matters is that we keep preaching.

> What matters is that we keep preaching. What matters is that we keep loving. What matters is that we say yes. What matters is that we are faithful.

What matters is that we keep loving. What matters is that we say yes. What matters is that we are faithful.

NEXT TO YOU. NEXT TO ME.

It may shock you that I no longer wear my supercool Jamba Juice ensemble. However, years of shopping at thrift stores and learning how to sew allowed me to curate pieces that were unique to me, that I valued in a different way. I ended up falling in love with upcycling garments and later had closets of refurbished vintage clothes (that some of you mourned with me about a few chapters ago) and taught other friends how to create capsule wardrobes on a budget. I was able to help my friends living on the street who were preparing for job interviews dress proudly and professionally with hidden treasures I found at consignment shops. While I was living on the road, I was able to live out of two suitcases, constantly updating and hemming clothes and changing them up with new buttons and fabrics, as I already knew how to live a frugal, minimalistic life because of what I had learned as a kid. I was the aficionado of frugalness, the connoisseur of consignments stores, a thrift store BO$$ (but instead of dollar signs, put in cent symbols!).

It turns out, the things that made me unique as a kid, that I once disdained about myself, played key roles in the skills I needed to serve others and obey God's call when I got older. I still use all these skills today. It turns out, being myself is far more freeing and far more fun. I may not look like other people, have skills like other people, or have a background like other people, but in God's kingdom, there is a place for me. Everything that was in front of me, He wanted to use.

Like those who rebuilt the city of Jerusalem, say yes to what's in front of you. Nehemiah listed the priests who lined up next to one another to repair the wall in front of them: "Next to them, Zadok son of Immer made repairs opposite his house. Next to him, Shemaiah son of Shekaniah, the guard at the East Gate, made repairs" (3:29 NIV).

And it continues. *Next to them, next to him, or the next section* is found in the story over twenty times. It took the whole community together. No one could sit this out.

It will take Dominic writing songs, next to Yolanda writing books, next to Alberto being kind to the patients he nurses, next to Amelia building shelves for her school, next to Mishka encouraging the kids she nannies, next to Dennis offering to mow his neighbors' lawns, next to Mike writing small-group curriculum, next to Natalie being gracious toward her employees, next to large churches, next to small churches, next to urban ministries on the streets, next to speakers in stadiums, next to preachers in parks, next to poets purchasing Oreo cakes in markets.

Next to you, next to your kids, next to your family.

Right where you are, there's a place for you. There's a need for you. And there's a need for the person right next to you. What God wants to do in our lives and our world won't be accomplished if we're comparing ourselves to one another. We are all needed to rebuild and repair the city.

> Right where you are, there's a place for you.

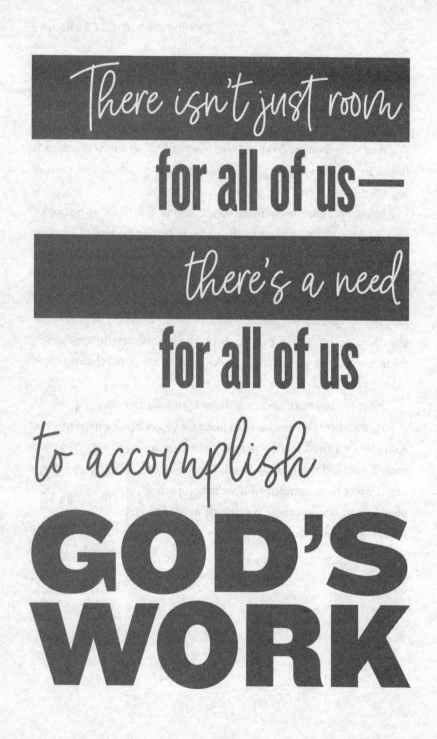

How (not) to Save the World

#10 | Always Fly Solo

It would be more than four years before I would have my own address. As a guest in people's homes, I'd frequently sleep on couches, cots, and twin-size beds in children's rooms as the selfless toddlers would stay with their parents for the night. Once a sweet little girl put all of her stuffed animals around the bed for me and said they'd protect me (that stuffed fuchsia unicorn *did* look threatening). I became a seasoned expert at packing and unpacking my torn-up plum leather suitcase in a moment's notice, a hurried blur leaving cities as quickly as I arrived. I never wanted to overstay my welcome. I never wanted to be a burden.

Early on I met Sean and Shelley.

I was performing at an event a few hours from where they lived when Sean, a creative arts pastor at his church, asked if I'd be interested in performing every weekend for their upcoming five-week church series. I'd be staying in a guest room in their home.

From the moment they and their three beautiful daughters opened their olive-green door to invite me in, they treated me like family. They were now making each meal for six, inviting me to their daughter's school functions, and frequently asking me about my life, family, and "what's next" plans.

The more hospitable they were toward me, the more insane I thought they were. I was not interested in letting these strangers in. I didn't need their help or their pity—I knew how to survive on my own. I was just here for work. I tried to keep them at arm's length.

On the streets I grew up on, you had to fend for yourself. When my dad died, I had to take care of myself. Paying for college, all I had was myself. When I made the decision to go on the road, I had never felt less supported and more alone, but I was a fighter. I had proven to myself over and over again that I could do more things alone than most people could. Letting people in would slow me down, and I was leaving their house in a month anyway.

It took me years to realize what I wish I had known my whole life: Always flying solo? That's how (not) to save the world. This lie has been one of the loudest in my life. The truth is that we alone will never fulfill God's full purposes for our lives and become who He has made us to be. We are not Han. We were never meant to do this Solo. (Had to. Not sorry. No regrets.)

A couple of weeks into my stay, their girls already in bed, Sean, Shelley, and I sat around their flickering fireplace. The aroma of butter and chocolate filled the air as we ate some of Shelley's delicious home-baked cookies. After kind words of their love for me, how they saw me like family and wanted to know me more, they tearfully asked, "Why won't you let us in?"

I froze. Where to begin?

Have you ever resisted letting people in? Have you ever tried as best as you could to avoid engaging in community?

Community is a difficult thing. Pastors preach on it well, church series address it well, and for the most part we get that it's a positive thing, a desired addition by many. But many of us have been connected to a community that deeply hurt us, and we're not excited about diving headfirst again into yet another unexplored ocean of vulnerability. We don't want our hearts to hope for or invest in something that will just be snatched away. We don't want to trust the wrong people. And we know we can survive alone if we have to.

When the Creator of the universe first thought of us and hand-made us, He designed us to be in community—*with* God and *with* each other. Community is not an optional add-on in our Amazon cart that we can choose before we check out the main items. It's essential for our lives to reach their full potential. Community empowers us not only to complete the tasks God has called us to but to become the people He has made us to be.

The Enemy knows this. And he's playing his hand as best he can to eliminate any threat to his plans of division and depravity. Frankly, he's playing it how I would.

If I were the Enemy, and my goal was for people to never access the full life available to them and never live out the purpose God has for them,

- I would throw any possible division I could to keep people far from community;
- I would speak lie after lie to people about how they don't need community or why they can't possibly have community, about how they're below and disqualified from having a community, or why they are above or too good for having a community;

- I would try to instill within them exclusive standards and snobbish expectations for a community so they wouldn't see the real people truly available to them;
- and anytime someone would consider the risk of letting a person into the vulnerable places of their heart, I would whisper, "Remember the last time you did this? Remember how hurt you were by community?" I would use any old wound and fear I could to keep God's people from living the lives we were made to live.

The Enemy is a liar. It's time to expose his lies. It's time to stop listening to them. It's time to shine truth on our soul's true need for people we can do life with.

A NEW KIND OF COMMUNITY

I deeply loved the church on the streets where I grew up. But as I visited my high school friends' churches, I realized they were not the same. Not just that people weren't drinking alcohol or shooting up cocaine during the services, *that part* was a given. It was more than that. I felt like many were putting on facades, pretending to be someone they were not. I couldn't figure out how to get to know people because I couldn't tell who people really were. The cliques were far too cool for me, and I wasn't at all sure who really loved Jesus or even liked people.

In college, I was surrounded by several students pursuing professional Christendom—they were in school to be pastors, worship leaders, and missionaries—and yet some of them were the most judgmental people I had ever met, their gossip some of the cruelest I had ever heard. I spent my entire childhood getting to know Jesus and His love for people and had no interest in some other version of Him, the one these people served. This community was not for me. As Ariana Grande would say, "thank u, next."[1]

Sean and Shelley disrupted my critical, closed-off way of thinking. They opened up a whole new world of possibilities of what a real community could actually be like. From their selfless invitations to host whatever parties their friends had coming up, to volunteering to decorate or organize any church event and making it a fun, family activity, to their refreshingly vulnerable Bible studies during the week with other families, their home was always open. They were the same people at church that they were at work, to their neighbors, to people close to them, to those close to Jesus, and to those who didn't know God at all. They weren't exclusive. The whole neighborhood was always invited. And so was this traveling twentysomething they hardly knew who needed a place to stay for the month.

I realized not only what community *could* be, but that I could be a part of creating a community that looked like what a real, Jesus-centered community looks like. A community without shame, without elitism, and without exclusivity. A community of authentic Jesus-followers who are not perfect but who love one another anyway.

The Word of God is flooded with truths about what a real Jesus-centered community looks like.

- We are called to be kind to one another and forgive one another (Eph. 4:32). Jesus does not shame people, so neither do we.
- We are called to love one another as God has loved us (1 John 4:11). As we do, God's love lives within us and "God's love has accomplished its mission among us" (1 John 4:12).

- We are called to not let anyone or anything cause division among us (1 Cor. 1:10). The world may love division and drama and gossip, holding on to old hurts and hoping for vengeance against others, but we don't. A Jesus-centered community is about restoration, reconciliation, and being unified together.
- We are called to continuously encourage one another, motivate one another toward more acts of love, and keep gathering together as community (Heb. 10:24–25). Now is not the time to pull away from community. Now is the time to be the church that God calls us to be. Now is the time to create the kind of community that truly looks like Jesus.

More than ever, we need to be unified and hardcore about coming together.

As I opened up to Sean and Shelley and allowed them into the once-closed walls of my heart, I realized I *could* do life alone, but I *could not* obey God to the best of my ability without letting real friendships in.

> Now is the time to create the kind of community that truly looks like Jesus.

When I was believing lies about myself, feeling like I wasn't good enough, they spoke truth to me. When I didn't know how to design a website, Sean helped me. When I didn't know how to stay positive amid pain, Shelley showed me. When I needed help selling my CDs at a small open mic down the road, their girls came and helped me. I could not only accomplish more *through my life* with people, but my actual *day-to-day life* was more purpose-filled and, frankly, more fun.

I'd been so focused on what God wanted me to do that I had paid little attention to who He wanted me to be. Once I knew the healing that came from community, I did not want to miss it. I wanted to be more open to it. How healed could I be? How enjoyable could this life be? How much more purpose could I step into? I wanted it all.

This did *not* turn this introvert into an extrovert. I was still me. This didn't make me blindly trust just anyone or allow any passerby into the inner workings of my heart. I was still wiser and more discerning than I had been in the past. But my determination to do life alone was fading. I was more determined now to be the best version of myself. To glorify God as best as I could with my life. And now the Enemy's lies were being exposed. The truth was that I needed a Jesus-focused community in order to thrive.

ACCEPT AND ASK

With Sean and Shelley, I accepted the invitation to be welcomed into a community I never dreamed of. Sometimes we need to receive what God is offering us. But sometimes we need to ask for the community we've been hoping for. Sometimes we need to pursue the answers to our prayers.

With Lori, I asked.

For me, an all-time champion of doing life alone, pursuing Lori was an exception to every relationship I had prior to that point in my life. I met her at a church that invited me to perform at their youth event. She was kind and welcoming. But being the senior pastor's wife, the founder of a large ministry that empowers other women in ministry,[a] an author, and a mom of two kids, she couldn't have been a busier person. Plus, we were not in the same life phase. On paper, we were an unlikely pair.

Our first lunch together was a huge step for me. Lori didn't know I

---

a. Leadingandlovingit.com. All women in ministry: preachers, writers, leaders, church staff, creatives, starters, and boss ladies—check it out and get connected! You won't regret it.

had never reached out to someone like this before, and there was no way for either of us to know that we would stay in touch over the years as I continued to travel from city to city, as her ministry continued to grow and evolve, as we wrote books of similar titles and themes at the same time and laughed the whole time, texting each other during the writing process, as I flew into her town to watch a season premiere of a shared favorite reality show (no one is perfect, Jesus is still working on us), and as she always planned adventure-filled outings with groups of friends whenever I was passing through her state. We kept in touch, we stayed consistent, we both invited, accepted, and had lots of long conversations (both our husbands are glad we've found each other), and we began to trust each other with the inner workings of our ministries and lives.

When my heart was shattered through a painful and unjust season in ministry, I was again tempted to build my walls back up. But this time, I knew better. The Enemy had victory over this part of me once before. I wasn't going to let him win again. He may have thought he had the victory through this hurtful situation, but if I let people into my hurt, to speak truth to his lies, he couldn't win the battle over my mind. I was not going to believe the lie again that I was better off alone.

Lori was the first friend I entrusted the pain of this season to. I wept as we sat on the warm sand of Venice Beach, California, the loud crashing waves unable to hide the volume of my sobs. My heart was fully exposed. I had never before been this vulnerable, broken, and messy in front of Lori. I was embarrassed. I was heartbroken. I felt like a failure. She simply held me in her arms. She was on my side. She was going to go through this with me. I was not alone. She and her closest friends rallied around me and spoke so much truth into my life. I walked through that season with greater faith and a greater sense of purpose than I ever could have had alone. Our trust in each other was strengthening, and what was once a friendship became a sisterhood.

That moment on the beach was four years after I had met Lori. Years later, she's one of my very best friends in the world.

Close relationships are not built overnight. They take consistency and vulnerability. And they are rarely forced. When God puts someone in your life, on your heart, or consistently on your mind, don't ignore it. Don't dismiss it because it's not the community you had in mind. If you do, you will miss out on the various life-giving relationships around you that can build and strengthen you. And don't put pressure on every lunch date to be your lifelong confidant. Friendships at various levels and in various seasons are valuable. Some come out of nowhere. Some might surprise you.

For many of us, the first step is reaching out to one person, whether that's accepting or asking. Is there someone who has invited you that you can say yes to? Is there someone who comes to mind that you could have the courage to reach out to? It may not be the best friend you've dreamed of since you were nine. It may not be the exact community that you'll have in fifteen years. Resist the temptation to limit what God wants to do in and through your life and through His people based on your preferred timelines and limited expectations.

Many of us have said, "There's no one I can reach out to," though there are people at our church we've never even tried to ask out to coffee. We've said, "Well, no groups invite me to anything," when we are not actively inviting people to things ourselves. We've said, "There's no one who understands me in my local community," though there's a world of people we've met throughout the years—and we still have their numbers or are friends with them on Facebook—who we have all the power to message.

Many people in your local community feel like no one understands *them*. (Look! You already have something in common!) For many of us the first step is to start accepting and start asking. Don't put the pressure on every relationship to be your new partner in crime, ride or die, Klay Thompson to your Steph Curry. Decide that your purpose is worth activating, and since community strengthens it, it's worth taking a risk for and a step toward.

The Enemy hopes we do life alone. He hopes we puff out our chests, raise our wounds high, and sing our egotistical anthems of how we can live our days alone. He hopes we stand on pompous pedestals of our personality test results and all the reasons why certain communities will work but others won't, and all the excuses of why we're better off flying solo. Though we know we were handmade by God to thrive in community, the Enemy hopes we try to maneuver around God's best, find watered-down alternatives of living, and settle for lives that never fulfill God's purposes and never threaten the Enemy's plans. If you want to keep settling, keep doing life alone. Just know that you won't grow into who you were created to be. God's purpose for our lives includes our being in community.

> **God's purpose for our lives includes our being in community.**

FOREVER LIVING

Growing up in the Bay Area, my family didn't have to drive too far to come across an entire forest of redwood trees. My elementary school would frequently take us on field trips to learn the intricacies of these tall, strong, and beautiful creations that seemed to reach to the sky. I learned that redwoods are the some of the tallest, strongest trees in the world. Their Latin name means "forever living," and they're so resilient that storms are typically no match for them.

The fascinating thing about these redwoods is that their roots don't even run that deep. They are only that strong and only have such an impressive lifespan because their roots intertwine with other surrounding redwood trees. Alone, a redwood won't grow as tall and can at times be blown over by intense weather. However, in a forest of redwoods, underneath the soil's surface, there are millions of connected roots, each helping to hold up one another. Supported redwoods can survive storms because they are intricately locked in with one another.

The same is true of us, the community of the church. If we decide to do life all alone, we will never be our best. When the raging storms come, they won't find us at our strongest.

In the Word of God, we see many names for the community of believers.

- We are called a *family* (Rom. 8:14–17; Eph. 2:17–19). In a family, you share an identity and a name. You share a heritage. When we choose Jesus, we are adopted into the family of God, and we all receive the inheritance that comes from being a part of this family.
- We are called a *temple* (Eph. 2:21–22; 1 Pet. 2:4–10). Centered around Jesus, we are all different pieces that come together to hold up one another and to build an atmosphere to worship the one true God.
- We are called a *flock of sheep* (John 10:1–18). We are cared for by the same Shepherd. We are a part of the same flock. He cares for all of us. He'll go out of His way to save and protect any of us and bring us back to where we belong.
- We are called a *body* (1 Cor. 12:12–17). We are meant to function as one entity, in one spirit, with one goal. Still, we are all different parts of this being, and none of our purposes or functions are like any other's. We need eyes on our faces, but we're

not all eyes. We need veins inside our bodies, but we're not all veins. We need feet, but *thank God* we're not all feet! We each have different jobs, different roles, and, just like a body, not all of our functions are visible. But we all have a vital purpose and function in the Body of Christ.

- We are called *branches* (John 15:1–8). We're the most productive when we're connected to the source of life: Jesus. He is the Vine. As we stay connected to Him, we produce powerful things. As we *all* stay connected to Him, remaining in Him and receiving life from Him, there is no telling what wondrous fruit we'll all produce together.

- We are called *Christ's bride* (Rev. 19:7–8). The church is the love of Jesus' life. He gave up His life for us. He defends us. He fights for us. He adores us. We have a sacred place in His heart.

The church is Jesus' plan to reach a world that desperately needs Him. The lost have hope through it. The hurt are healed through it. We must love and forgive and fight to protect it because the community of the church is His absolute favorite. Alone, we cannot expect to be victorious in our battle against darkness. Alone, we cannot expect to stand tall through raging storms. Alone, we can't expect to rebuild our cities and restore our communities. To walk in our purposes and to stay on mission, we must walk with other people and stay in community. The more unified we are, the greater our impact will be. This will take accepting invitations. And this will take making invitations. This might take opening up our hearts by fireplaces and crying along sandy beaches. This might take embracing a community in front of you or, perhaps, creating the community you've longed for.

To walk in your **PURPOSE** and stay on **MISSION,** walk with other **PEOPLE** and stay in **COMMUNITY**

How (not) to Save the World

#11 | Pick Your Favorites

My ten-year-old niece, Eden, put me in my place. She texted me a link to a short video on social media of a girl dancing. The trend of learning dance moves to popular songs was on the rise and she was one of its earliest fans. Soon after, she FaceTimed me saying, "Auntie, I thought this was you! I watched so many videos from this girl before I realized it was *not* you!"

Thinking I could joke with her and convince her it *was* me, I smugly teased, "That girl looks just like me! That girl dresses just like me! How do you know that's not me?"

My niece, who is too intelligent for her own good and would not be tricked, immediately laughed, saying, "I realized it was not you once I remembered that you can't dance!"

Wow. Thanks, kid. Clearly, *words of affirmation* is not her love language.

This girl we were watching resembled me. She had similar

characteristics to me. Quite frankly, it was shocking. But to Eden, the definitive difference between me and this girl was how we acted—how we moved and especially how we danced. Once she saw the difference in our actions, she realized we were not the same.

ACTUALLY FOLLOWING JESUS

Jesus' brother James was alarmed at how early Christ-followers preached one way but lived another way entirely. They resembled Christ. They spoke some of the same words as Christ. You could tell there were similarities. But they did not act like Him. James asked his fellow believers, "How can you claim to have faith in our glorious Lord Jesus Christ if you favor some people over others?" (James 2:1 NLT).

James realized that many enjoyed being a part of the *Jesus religion* but did not want to live the *Jesus way*, being welcoming and inclusive like Him, loving like Him, and working toward unity like He did. They loved to say they were people of faith, but that was not evident in how they treated others. It was all talk, all show, all spectacle, and not Jesus. James was alerting those who claimed to follow Christ: "You can't have *real* faith in Jesus and also favor a group of people above another." The distinction is too clear. The two actions do not match up.

James continued, talking about a rich person getting preferred treatment in church over someone with lesser means and the discrimination that demonstrates (2:2–4). Maybe you and I can't relate to treating rich people better than less-affluent people when they step into our church buildings, but maybe we can relate to wanting to be around the most popular kids at school and staying far away from the less popular or strategizing on how to go out to dinner with people with greater networks and large social media followings, well-connected people who can advance our careers, while avoiding going out to coffee with people who may be in need of community but who can't contribute to our careers at all. Maybe when you're hiring someone, you are partial to choosing people with your background or skin color or race. Perhaps you try to curate friend groups filled with those only of a certain financial status or particular level of influence.

James was saying that doesn't line up with how to act like Jesus. If we don't care about loving like Jesus did, what do we think following Jesus is?

James reminded Christ-followers of Jesus' clear commandment of love and the actual calling that comes from Him. "*Remember His call, and* live by the royal law found in Scripture: love others as you love yourself. You'll be doing very well if you can get this down. But if you show favoritism—*paying attention to those who can help you in some way, while ignoring those who seem to need all the help*—you'll be sinning and condemned by the law" (2:8–9).

> If we don't care about loving like Jesus did, what do we think following Jesus is?

Jesus came into this broken world to tell everyone how loved and valuable they are. He came to destroy labels, walls, barriers, and divisions caused by the sin of hate and the sin of prejudice. He also came to restore what's been broken inside of us, between us, and between us and God. Jesus' mission was a mission of reconciliation. We know "He charges us to proclaim the message that heals and restores our broken relationships *with God and each other*" (2 Cor. 5:19). The Jesus mission is not a mission of division. It is not a mission of picking who to love, who is worthy of our compassion, who is worthy of our kindness, and who is worthy of our respect. It's a mission of letting everyone know they are invited.

But others throughout history have loved labels, barriers, and divisions. That's the anti-Jesus mission. Sadly, these divisions and labels have found their way into church history as well. Jesus people haven't always gotten this one right. They weren't always getting it right in the first generation of the church either. That's why Jesus spoke about this so much. It was important to Him. It's why James spoke about it in these verses. It's why we're talking about it today. Our culture has the same problems. We like picking favorites. Our bias can feel so natural, *how can it be wrong?* The rest of the world does it all the time! Magazines love their lists of who is more important than whom. The media loves worshipping certain humans because of external factors and disregarding others that seem less impressive. The world loves its Top 100 lists, its exclusive clubs, and all its impressive categories. *Is choosing my favorite people to love and respect actually so wrong?*

It is.

James was asking the community of the church: "How could you have faith in the One who came to unify and yet be causing all this division, working against His mission? Your actions do not line up."

Picking favorites? That's how (not) to save the world.

Paul reminded us: "God does not play favorites" (Rom. 2:11 GW).

If God does not pick and choose which human is more valuable than another, then who do we think *we* are?

When we look down on someone and think less of their life's value because of their race, background, economic state, job status, marital status, clothes, body size, or any other external factor, we are not just saying we think we are greater than that human, we are also saying that we think we are greater than God. Do we think we have more authority to decide the value of human life, more than the One who created human life? Perhaps this is not a question of "How do you see others?" Perhaps the question is: "How do you see God?"

What is the sin inside of me that causes me to think I have more authority than the One who created me? What is torn inside of me that makes me think that I can degrade someone made in imago Dei, in God's own image?

For many of us, this is where we need to begin. We need to take time alone with God and pray as the psalmist prayed, "Investigate my life, O God, find out everything about me; Cross-examine and test me, get a clear picture of what I'm about; See for yourself whether I've done anything wrong—then guide me on the road to eternal life" (Ps. 139:23–24 MSG).

Picking favorites is not saving the world. It is breaking apart our world and working against what Jesus came to accomplish. It's time to identify our bias. It's time to get honest about who we ultimately see God as.

THE JESUS WAY

While Jesus walked on the earth, He condemned the legalistic people of His day—the ones who were more concerned about outward religious rituals than welcoming and serving *people*. He was not against adhering to sacred traditions but made it clear that they were not the matters to be the most concerned about. He revealed the Pharisees' hypocritical ways: "You are fastidious about tithing—keeping account of every little leaf of mint and herb—but you neglect what really matters: justice and the love of God!" (Luke 11:42).

The Pharisees were not necessarily bad people; they were actually a lot like us—well-intentioned and wanting to obey God. But they took a detour. They went from holding on to the worship of God to holding on to rules.

Some of us have been taught to believe that our faith is defined by going to church on Sunday, being in a small group on a Wednesday, tithing, watching Christian movies, and sharing Bible verses on Facebook. None of these things are bad things! I do all of these things, and I enjoy doing them. But Jesus made it clear—these are not the *most important things*. He noted what really matters: justice and the love of God. The Pharisees were perhaps like many of us, knowing how to live the culturally Christian way but not always living the actual Jesus way.

Does this mean Jesus cares more about our fighting for justice for others and loving people where they are than tithing our income, organizing worship services, and attending powerful Christian events? I mean . . . that's a bit harsh. I did not say that. But Jesus did.

Let me be clear—these other practices matter *a lot*. Note that Jesus said, "You should tithe, yes, but do not neglect the more important things" (Luke 11:42 NLT). Tithing to your local church is important. It is *also* a God-honoring act of obedience. Jesus just wants us to know the order of His priorities. He knew that from time to time we would get it wrong. He wanted to make sure we remembered: loving people is His priority.

Jesus did not only condemn the pious, religious people, He also condemned the culturally intellectual. The smart ones. The educated ones. The ones who perhaps chose knowledge as an idol over people as a priority. Jesus said to them, "You load other people down with unbearable burdens *of rules and regulations*, but you don't lift a finger to help others" (Luke 11:46).

Does that sound like any of us? Have we ever been quicker to condemn someone's moral behavior than to ask how they are and how we can be there for them? Have we ever written witty rebuttals on Twitter, cleverly condemning people not living up to our moral code, meanwhile not writing or speaking in the loving way Jesus has asked us to speak to others? Have we ever preached to our kids or little brothers and sisters about all the things that are *wrong* to do, without leading them and encouraging them in the things that are *right* to do? Have we sat with them and talked about having loving relationships with those not like them, how to include those whom others exclude, those who are bullied, those who are overlooked, and how to actively love and serve others? Have we demonstrated what a life of humility and service looks like? Have we spoken to them about the issues Jesus cared most about—justice and God's love?

For many of us, our priorities are good, even holy, and rooted in obedience to God. Sometimes they are just in the wrong order.

I want to spend my life following Jesus. I want to actively seek out the unjust practices and systems in my own career, community, city, and world and discover how I can be a part of the solution. I want to care about what Jesus cared about first. Justice and love. It may not look like what other Christians think should be my priority, but a Christ-follower is a follower of Christ. Not a follower of Christians.

Instead, I want to love what God loves, and I want to hate what God hates.

For many of us, this is counterintuitive to what we may have thought about God. We may think, *God doesn't hate.* And that may sound sweet and spiritual. But it is not biblical.

> **A Christ-follower is a follower of Christ. Not a follower of Christians.**

We read in Proverbs 6:16–19:

> *Take note,* there are six things the Eternal hates; no, *make it* seven
> He abhors: Eyes that look down on others, a tongue that can't be

trusted, hands that shed innocent blood, A heart that conceives evil plans, feet that sprint toward evil, A false witness who breathes out lies, and anyone who stirs up trouble among the faithful.

God loves every person. But because He loves *everyone*, He can't love *everything* because some things hurt the ones He loves. We have heard it said before that love is not a feeling, love is an action. That means, then, there are times when we show no action that we are not living in love. Jesus-followers: We don't want to be a community known for our feelings. We want to be a community known for our love. This means we must be a community of action.

If this is what God hates, then let's flip it to see what God loves.

- If God hates eyes that look down on others, He must love when we value others and actively lift them up. How can you lift someone up today? How can you let someone know that you value them?

- If God hates a tongue that cannot be trusted, He must love when we tell the truth, when we are honest with ourselves and with others. How can we have trusted tongues? How can we commit to reading the Word of God consistently, speaking only what is true to what God says? How can we be introspective about the ways that we could be wrong so we are continuously living and speaking honestly?

- If God hates hands that shed innocent blood, He must love when our hands and our actions are used to prevent innocent blood from ever being shed. In what ways are we actively speaking against and continuously praying against the sins and evils of human hearts that take an innocent human being's life?

- If God hates a heart that conceives evil plans and feet that sprint toward evil, He must love hearts that come up with healing plans and feet that run toward whatever brings people to Jesus. What is a plan you will make that will lead people toward their true, valued identity in Christ? What solutions are you running toward for God's people to know the truth of who they are? For the welcoming and restoring of people: What is your plan?
- If God hates a false witness who breathes out lies and anyone who stirs up trouble among the faithful, He must love a witness of the truth who says what God says, who lives by what God says—not just what our culture says—and who actively stirs up unity among God's children. What ways have you been speaking on behalf of what the world loves and what the world hates? What ways have you stirred division among people? Instead, what ways can you rally up a sense of unity?

I am not saying any of this will be easy. I am saying that, at its core, this is what a life following Jesus is: a reconciled relationship with Him and a reconciled relationship with others.

So let's talk about our hearts. And let's talk about our day-to-day lives. In your place of work, in your group of friends, in the way you speak to strangers, in the way you post online, is there a bias you operate in that you need to lay before God?

We need to leave behind the ways the Enemy has had victory in our bias and instead say to God, "I want to love what You love. I want to hate what You hate."

It's time for us to surrender. It's time for us to turn away from the sin in our hearts that makes us play God and pick favorites. It's time to turn toward Jesus and join Him on His mission of reconciliation.

DANCE LIKE ME

Eden encouraged me, "Auntie, you can learn how to dance like this girl if you want to! I'll show you! You keep watching her over and over, and practice her moves, and then you dance the same way!" She went on to tell me the hours she spent staring at and learning the dance moves herself, the focus and time invested into moving like these online stars, and then proceeded to show me her newfound skills. Hands posed in the air. The music began. She knew every single move.

Jesus gives us a similar invitation.

If we choose to follow Him, focus on Him, and put intentional time and practice into learning His ways, we will move like He moves.

Jesus said, "Everyone will know you as My followers if you demonstrate your love to others" (John 13:35).

Just like my niece noticed, the definitive difference between me and this dancer was our actions. The sad reality is that we can quite quickly come off like we represent Jesus, but the truth of who we are actually following will eventually be revealed through how we live our lives.

I wish there was a download into my brain so that I could instantly dance how this girl danced, or at least an app that would move my limbs for me and control me as if I were Pinocchio. (A girl version though. Pinocchia.) Instead, it will take focus and consistent practice.

> The world will not know we follow Jesus by our merely preaching amazing love. The world will know we follow Jesus when we practice actual love.

Living like Jesus is also not an instant download. We do not choose Him and then all of a sudden know perfectly how to love like Him. He invites us to look at Him. And keep looking at Him. Spend time with Him. Read His Word. Practice moving like Him. Over time we will get the hang of it, and we will begin to live like Him. People will see us and know that we have spent time with Him.

The world will not know we follow Jesus by our merely preaching amazing love. The world will know we follow Jesus when we practice actual love.

A START

We want to turn away from our bias. We want to turn toward Jesus. And then we want to keep practicing living like Him day by day. Today is a great day to start. Today, we will not master how to actively love every person perfectly. Today, we will not solve all the world's problems. But today we can make the choice to say, *We will not be overwhelmed by the brokenness of our world to the point where we do nothing.* We will come to God and say: *My whole life is about knowing, loving, and following You. May I love what You love and hate what You hate. Show me how to specifically partner with You on Your mission. I turn toward You. I'm looking at You. And today, I want to start.*

- Maybe you're a parent and your starting point is raising kids who know from a young age how to see the world and love the world like Jesus would. That can look like reading specific books with them or having intentional conversations with them.
- Perhaps you're an entrepreneur and your starting point is to reevaluate some of the systems in your company so there's no favoritism or bias throughout your employees and clients,

aiming to run your business like Jesus would if He were in your shoes.

- Maybe you're passionate about graphic design and connecting through social media, and you've noticed how hurtful people can be online toward people not like them. You might start by being the change you want to see on social media, being purposeful and gracious with how you comment, what you post, the graphics you make, and how, by example, you lead your friends to also be more like Jesus would be on social media.

- Maybe you have always wanted for there to be a place in your community where people could gather, invite their friends—people who know God and people who don't, people who are like one another and people who aren't—and have a meal together. Maybe your starting point is planning a dinner party either at your house or at a restaurant. It may not be perfect. But today you can text a friend and ask if they want to join you in this dream. With the goal to welcome and include, today is a great day to start.

I do not know what your starting point is, but I know that if we are committed to being true Christ-followers then we must actively love what He loves. Jesus loves people more than anything. Every person. Every race. Every skin tone. Every gender. Every class. Loving every person like Jesus does is the most distinctive characteristic of Jesus people.

> Loving every person like Jesus does is the most distinctive characteristic of Jesus people.

A message of Jesus that excludes, divides, and devalues human lives is no Jesus message at all. The truth is that every single human is so crazy valuable and important to God. And when we rank, worship, or devalue His people, we are joining with the Enemy in his plan to destroy and tear apart and fight against Jesus' mission to unite.

We know that when our earthly lives come to an end and we're spending eternity with God, there won't be just us and the people we know but a "vast crowd, too great to count, from every nation and tribe and people and language, standing in front of the throne and before the Lamb" (Rev. 7:9 NLT). And just as Jesus did with His friends while He was on earth, sitting at tables, and eating good food—that's what He says He'll do with us. Every tribe, every nation, an all-powerful God, and a delicious meal.

Jesus Himself said this: "People will come from the East and the West—*and those who recognize Me, regardless of their lineage, will sit with Me at that feast*" (Matt. 8:11).

Do not settle for the value systems of the world. Don't aim for a community that looks like earth. Aim for a community that looks like heaven. Every single human has been created in the image of God, and there is room at the table for every single one of us. Jesus calls us to make sure that everyone knows they are invited to that table.

Choose to **LOVE** & **VALUE** *every person* *like* **JESUS DOES**

How (not) to Save the World

#12 | Despise the Bride

I was once given a speaking honorarium in used Starbucks cards. After I taught at two church services on Sunday morning, the pastor handed me the two green-and-white plastic cards, both marked as being fifty dollars. I was grateful. You can get a lot of savory goodies at the 'Bucks for one hundred dollars, and this gift was sure to provide breakfast and coffee for a week or two. This was no small deal.

After services I had about a six-hour drive ahead of me before reaching my next destination. The snack life was about to go *down*.

I slapped the wide, black handle, opening the door to the inviting aromas of Pike Place Roast brewing. I ordered an oatmeal, a hot black coffee—venti (let he who is without sin cast the first stone)—and for an extra treat and road-trip sustenance, I added in a Naked Juice and warm, buttery croissant. I was living it up this Sunday! To my disappointment, when I handed the barista a card, I learned that one of them had only $12.37 left on it.

Womp womp.

With my head held down I whispered, "Just the coffee and oatmeal, please."

I had a long week ahead of me and needed to make those cards last. I headed out to the next city with a mixture of gratitude, disappointment, and the tingling taste of brown sugar in my oatmeal to soften some of the blow. Sugar can do that. And it comes from the Almighty. (And all of God's people said, "amen.")

I've had greater hurt in the church than this. My guess is you have too.

Worse than a gift card being a bit short of what was promised, we've had people we care about speak one way to our faces and another way about us behind our backs. We've sincerely tried to connect with various groups of people, searching for genuine friendships, and have been made to feel less than or unworthy whenever we're not invited to the party or not included at the event. We have had our hopes and expectations high, imagining what the community of the church could be like, only to be disappointed time and time again, shortchanged from what we felt was promised.

We thought this entire community would always be welcoming, kind, inviting, and consistent. Perfect reflections of Jesus, right? Never speaking ill of us, always providing for us, and regularly keeping our faith in humanity. Instead, what we thought would be $100 worth of holy and healing relationships turned out to be a disappointing $62.37 of cliques, competition, ego-strutting, and broken promises. We feel a mixture of gratitude and hurt and are in dire need of some sugar.

THE PROBLEM

When we have expectations for other humans to be little saviors and put broken people on pedestals to be the answers to our deepest needs, we will be greatly disappointed. Humans are horrible saviors.

As we dwell on these hurts of feeling mistreated or ignored, steam seeps out as bitterness boils within us. We go round and round in gossipy cul-de-sacs, alerting the neighborhood and hoping other people disdain the same people we do. We crash like wrecking balls into the reputations of our leaders, hoping to tear down their credibility and alarm others of how very human those they looked up to turned out to be. Sometimes we march out of the church altogether in protest because we can't stand "those people."

In the blink of an eye, we start to despise the bride. And I promise you: that's how (not) to save the world. Tearing down the love of Jesus' life is no way to show the love of Jesus to the world.

Though we are glad God made exceptions in our case, we wish He'd stop letting so many other broken and hurting people into His church. We had dreams of utopian communities, strictly sacred and inspiring conversations, and perfectly run organizations that would certainly be more enjoyable for us. If all the social ragamuffins and sinners would just stop breaking-and-entering our churches, demanding hope, forgiveness, and salvation for their souls, perhaps then we could have a more civilized spiritual community.

> Tearing down the love of Jesus' life is no way to show the love of Jesus to the world.

Instead, we are met with a group of people who are as broken, insecure, and hurting as we are. Attendees who care too much about what people think about them, like we do. Staff members who don't communicate perfectly, don't attend every event, and who fail at being perfect friends, like we do. These blaringly messy, real humans force us to give compassion to people who are not easy to love, to serve in areas that don't perfectly match up with our StrengthsFinder results, and to partner with people whose personalities clash with ours. And these sinners are exhausting. Who let them in? We want better bouncers standing at the back doors of our Christian club.

For many of us, loving destitute sinners on the side of the road like Jesus did—well, that's the easy part. Those people are clearly lost and must be found! But loving the sinners who are more like us, a bit more cleaned up and fairly faithful churchgoing people (but neither hurting nor holy enough for our standards), that's much more difficult.

In 1 Corinthians, Paul reminded the early churches of who *they* were when *they* were called. God didn't pick the most elite or most impressive. He chose the underdogs, the castoffs, the foolish, the basic, the not-so-basic, the uneducated, and the unpopular. Paul asked, "Isn't it obvious that God deliberately chose men and women that the culture overlooks and exploits and abuses, chose these 'nobodies' to expose the hollow pretensions of the 'somebodies'?" (1:27–28 MSG). This is good news for us when we remember we are the castoffs—those broken and sinful whom God has forgiven and chosen to bring His message to the world. We love being invited!

This becomes bad news when we want to approve the guest list, but remember how inclusive Jesus really is and realize He's also chosen the people we can't stand. God selected those who lack status, so none of us could brag that we have more qualifications than anyone else. The church *exposes* the grace and power of God. What makes it difficult is also what makes it amazing and unlike any other community in the world. The same grace that covers us has covered and invited all the other foolish nobodies too. Jesus is at the door, opening it wide and letting everybody in.

YOU AIN'T NO COVER GIRL

My wedding dress was ninety dollars at a consignment store.

Walking from my hotel room to a coffee shop before heading to a conference one humid August afternoon, I saw ivory and pearl-like vintage dresses peeking through a fogged glass window inside a mint, hole-in-the-wall boutique. I had about twenty to thirty minutes to spare and figured it was as good a time as any to go dress shopping. I was not the perfect bride. I did not take any time off of work or traveling to plan our wedding, so coming across stores mid-travel was the only way a dress was ever going to be bought or any decorations would be purchased. For the record, besides flowers, there were no decorations. I was decidedly too busy the several months before our wedding and deemed it not as important as my traveling schedule. If I could do it over, I likely would. And if you want to know how I somehow convinced an amazing guy named Guy to marry this crazy girl, you're going to have to wait a couple of chapters. Trust me, you'll love him.

I was not the perfect bride, but, boy, I loved this one dress. It was a few sizes too big, but I knew I could get it altered. There were large rips at the bottom, but I knew I could hem those myself, and there was a stain in the front-left corner that I knew I could add a layer of fabric over to conceal. It reminded me of something Judy Garland would wear strolling alongside Fred Astaire in *Easter Parade* or Debbie Reynolds while joyfully dancing beside Gene Kelly in *Singin' in the Rain*; both women weren't fancy to begin with, but with newfound confidence, and a glamorous gown, they transformed. I skipped out of the store with dress in hand, with just enough time to grab my coffee and bagel, before heading to speak.

Our wedding day wasn't all that traditional, and it certainly was not what many would deem "perfect." We had a barbecue with about thirty people in a backyard in the Bernal Heights district of San Francisco. We got married in the middle of the day with the smells of our friend grilling tri-tip floating in the air. I ran a bit late. I was wearing heels I had owned for years with tears in the buckle and some superglue pouring from the heel from a recent trip. (Not a road trip. A face trip.) I told the girl who came over to do my hair, "Do whatever you want!" Later, our wedding photographer would submit our photos to magazines and blogs, hoping to drum up more business, but they were never chosen and far from hitting the mark, as they lacked sufficient decorations and glamour and, as one magazine put it, had "no pizzazz."

I didn't have a Pinterest-worthy cascading bouquet of rare florals and fine ribbons, but instead a beautiful blossoming bunch of fresh dahlias, tied up with my dad's shoelaces. I ultimately still wanted him to walk me down the aisle, even in this imperfect way, and for his brown laces to be visible. I walked down a rickety wooden staircase instead of a linen-lined aisle to meet my soon-to-be-husband, who was smiling back at me with the biggest grin I'd ever seen. We stood in the middle of the small yard with our loyal, longtime friends, overlooking the cityscape of my hometown. I was not perfect. But I was the bride.

The church, the bride of Christ, is like every human who is a part of her—flawed, ripped up, and late. We're not perfect. We're not cover-worthy. We lack flash. We are not doing this as eloquently as we imagined we would. And this probably won't look like everyone else's idea of this sacred tradition.

She's no cover girl, but the bride is the love of Jesus' life. He's overjoyed at her arrival. The details of her dress or broken-down heels matter very little to Him. He always knew she'd run a little late and wouldn't put all that much thought into her hair. But she is who Jesus came for. Her presence is what He longs for. Their relationship is what He desires. Personally, we may have chosen a different venue, a more impressive guest list, a fancier menu, or an atmosphere with more . . . what's the word . . . *pizzazz*. But this isn't about you or your preferences. This is about the bride.

> She's no cover girl, but the bride is the love of Jesus' life.

Our churches are not places of Pinterest-board perfection. They are places of worship. It can be unappealing and frankly exhausting going to a place that is about building the kingdom of God and not a kingdom of you. Here, it's about Jesus. People aren't here to worship you, and you're not there to entertain them, but rather you are all coming together to draw close to the One who has saved all of you. The bride of Christ is not perfect—instead, it's real and filled with truly messy people saved by a life-changing grace. You're a part of that. I'm a part of that. Together, we are the imperfect bride, the love of Jesus' life.

It was about two months after my half-used Starbucks gift when I was invited to speak at an outreach to people without homes in a different state. Forty or so people on the street heard me share the gospel. That overcast, cloudy day reminded me of my growing up at the park on Jones and Eddy Streets. Afterward, the pastor handed me a gracious gift—larger than the $62.37 worth of gift cards I had recently received. He said they had been saving for months and felt like God had called them to take care of this young preacher girl. They also took an additional offering from the group of people sitting alongside the cement stairways and under the highway. I left with an additional

$3.12 in change. Truly a sacrifice for those who gave, and likely all they had. That gift left a greater impact on my life than they know.

I learned that day that the church was broken but also beautiful, and through God's family, He was going to take care of me. It wasn't going to be perfect. The Starbucks-enthusiast pastor was perhaps not the prime example of it. But I had a choice. I could focus on all that was wrong with the church, or I could focus on how I was being blessed by the church. I could choose if I wanted to be bitter because of a bad example of leadership or if I wanted to be better and go out of my way to serve people like the kind example I had seen under the overpass.

No matter the size of our resources, we can show up for the bride. We can show up for those in need. We can go above and beyond the examples given to us. We can be the sacrificial $3.12 worth of change we want to see in the world.

THE SOLUTION WITH A SIDE OF FRIES

When I was a little girl, my dad had a heartbreaking falling-out with a close friend and partner in ministry. It crushed him. Though they had at one point in time been like brothers, he had been deeply wounded, made to feel inadequate and less than, taken advantage of and connived against, and yet I would frequently overhear him in his bedroom in the morning praying for this relationship to be restored. He wrote letter after letter asking for the two of them to meet. Every no was more hurtful than the last. My family grieved with my dad. The cut was extremely deep.

One time, when I was in junior high, my dad took me after school to a McDonald's at a mall. As we sat down we saw the family of Dad's former close friend walking toward us from across the food court. Once our eyes met, they pivoted and walked to sit across the way. I had *quite* the attitude about it. I gave a whole speech to my dad about all the things I wanted to say them. "Oh, they *better* walk away!" I snapped with one hand while I ate my hot, steamy fries in the other. (McDonald's fries over any fry ever. Name a better fry. I'll wait.) I went on about what other people said about them, how my dad probably dodged a bullet, and how glad I was that they were out of our lives. My dad reached across the silver plastic table for my snapping, fryless hand and said, "Come on, let's go say hi."

Irritated and unsupportive, I let him drag me across the food court to where they sat. After brief hugs and shallow greetings, we walked back to our car. I noticed my dad's eyes welling up with tears as he opened the pale-brown car door. Noticing how upset he was, I implored, "Why did you do that? They were avoiding us. We didn't have to do that. You don't owe them anything."

He stopped midway through buckling his seat belt, looked me in the eyes and responded, "I know. I didn't do it for them."

He paused as he wiped a tear.

"I did it for you. I wanted you to see it. I want you to remember for the rest of your life that we're not like them. And we don't treat people based on how they treat us. We treat people based on how Jesus treated us. Do you understand me?"

"Yes, Dad."

He clicked on his seat belt, and we drove away.

I didn't think of that story again until my first real run of relational heartbreaks in the church. In one year's time, my heart had suffered more loss and betrayal than I ever thought was possible. My thoughts evolved from guilt—how gullible and weak I was to be taken advantage of so easily—to anger at how malicious other people were—to revengeful dreaming of the day I would aggressively defend myself and ultimately humiliate my offenders.

The Enemy loves it when we do his job for him. He loves it when the children of God tear apart other children of God. He loves when all of our energy and focus are geared toward tearing one another down so we don't spend one second building one another up and together accessing the purposes of God for our lives. He loves any moment he can kick off his shoes, sit back, and enjoy the children of God discouraging and hurting one another. Who doesn't love a day off?

> The Enemy loves it when we do his job for him. He loves it when the children of God tear apart other children of God.

Don't spend one second of your precious life helping the Enemy with his agenda. Don't divide. Don't tear down. Don't seek revenge. Don't make anyone feel less than the loved and purpose-filled child of God they are. Fight against the Enemy. Fight for people. Unify. Build up. Forgive. Speak life. This is how we will reveal God's love. This is how we will change the world.

At one point my hurts were so deep I thought with all my heart that I was going to walk away from the church completely. Even after I did all I could on my end to reconcile, forgive, and move forward, the walls of my heart were boarding up, afraid to let people in again, running from the risk of community.

In the midst of my heartache, on my knees weeping before the Lord, asking Him how this could happen to me and what I should do next, I remembered that moment in the McDonald's food court.

I am not like them.

When God sees how I walked through this season, I will not be found treating people based on how they treated me. I am called to more than circulating the hurt of other hurting people, like a nasty game of telephone, passing the pain on, each version of a story a little more elaborated on than the last. I am called to more than vindictive vendettas against God's people. I am called to be an agent of unity, an ambassador of reconciliation, a pioneer of real community amid a real hurting world.

Perhaps it was scrolling through spiteful posts on Facebook from once-avid-churchgoing, Jesus-loving people who were now saying nasty things about God's people, only to receive a choir of comments from people in agreement, publicly bashing their past leaders as if in a competition (not sure who the winners were). Perhaps it was a combination of watching heroes fall, leaders lie, loved ones leave, or lamenting how a watching world was hearing and seeing horrible depictions of Jesus and His people from Christians who cared little about the casualties of their hurtful actions. I can't recall the exact moment it happened. But it become clear to me. Change was only going to come from the inside.

The only way the church is going to be the community we are praying for is if people who really love Jesus stay in it and are His real representation from inside of it.

- We will not see change if we all just leave our ministries and constantly complain about all *those other people.*
- We will not see change if we keep going to new church after new church, constantly disapproving of their spiritual customer service and leaving a trail of hurtful tweets about all the inadequacies of all the senior leadership.
- We will not see change if we spend all of our time talking about, gossiping about, and posting about *those people.*

We will only see change within the church and broken lives truly healed in the name of Jesus if we say, *"We're the people.* We can be the change we've been praying for. We can be the leaders we've been begging God for. We can show people the beauty of the family of God.

> **We can be the change we've been praying for.**

We can be creators instead of critics. We can be builders instead of blamers. Someone needs to rise up. Let's go."

We want the church to be better at how they speak to one another, to stop gossiping, and to defend one another. We can be those people.

We want leaders who will fight for the marginalized and boldly stand against injustice. We can be those people.

We want the church to actually and actively love the people in our communities, lead with integrity, and stay in the dirt with people when it's hard. We can be those people.

It may not look like how we thought it would, and it will likely be as messy and imperfect as we punks who are pioneering it. And yet we can decide to not sit back and sulk but to instead stand up and lead.

God is searching the world for people who are desperate to know Him, to see the world like Him, to love others like Him. God is searching the world for people who love Jesus more than their egos and other people more than their paychecks. God is searching the world for people who are not just sticking to the status quo but instead feel called to raise the standard. And the people who can raise the standard in our communities are here. You and me. More than ever, I am determined to lead change from the inside. Join me. Let's show the world the real hope found in Jesus.

THE MISSION

I want to be clear. I am not talking about ignoring immoral behavior among our leaders. Or not standing up for the powerless and oppressed. Or dismissing hurt that's been done to you. Or not having a trusted group of friends and confidants who know you and love you and who you can share your hurts with. *Absolutely not.*

I am talking about the inside job many Christians, at times unknowingly, have signed on to that implodes God's plan A from the inside. Resist the urge to play into the Enemy's destructive agenda. Resist the temptation to burn God's house down. Don't degrade the very community you're called to grow. The church is better with you in it.

No matter our position or role, we all represent the beauty of the gospel of Jesus. It is not solely the responsibility of the senior leadership of your church to represent the bride of Christ to your community. Step up to the actual call that comes from Jesus. We are all openers of doors. We are all builders of tables. You are just as much what the world thinks of when they think of the church. Don't step back from it. Step up to it.

> The church is better with you in it.

I'm not saying it is easy. I am saying that a unified body of Christ is Jesus' rescue plan for a broken world. Jesus prayed that we would go together, unified, and as one (John 17:20–23). Best-case scenario? Those hurtful people will turn away from their divisive ways and join us on this mission. Restoration and reconciliation were always Jesus' plan. But if they don't join us, you and I still have a call from God on our lives. May we be the church Jesus prayed for.

- When you forgive those who hurt you instead of gossiping behind someone's back, you cancel the Enemy's plan.
- When you invite others, even when you feel uninvited, and welcome others, even when you feel unwelcomed, you cancel the Enemy's plan.

- When you pray for people, even *while* they are speaking ill of you, you cancel the Enemy's plan.
- When you step up to be the leader you've prayed for, the friend you've hoped for, and the mentor you've never had, you cancel the Enemy's plan.

With every moment of unity, building, and strengthening among God's people, Jesus is more glorified, and the Enemy is more afraid. With every door we open for people, a door for the Enemy slams shut.

Jesus said, "I will build my church. And the gates of hell will not overpower it" (Matt. 16:18 GW). If we want to fight against the gates of hell, we need to be unified together. No more self-serving smear campaigns. No more lane-swerving to cut off the call of God on others' lives. No more civil wars combatting your brothers and sisters. You were called to more.

Let's not fight against one another.

Let's fight against the gates of hell together.

THE CHURCH IS BETTER

WITH **YOU** in it

DON'T

TEAR DOWN THE VERY

COMMUNITY

you're called to

GROW

How (not) to Save the World

#13 | Fight the Wrong Battles

For years I held back the details of who I was in fear of what others would say about me. As I mentioned in earlier chapters, in fear of other people's opinions, I held back my obedience. I belittled my background. I held in my heritage. I silenced my story. It took me years to step out in faith toward what I felt God was calling me to. To see myself—a woman, the daughter of a recovered addict, and a multiracial Asian American—as made in His image. To know my story had a purpose and to use all I had gone through and all God had given me to serve His church and share His story as best as I could. Still, deep inside myself, I feared that one day the things that made me different would disqualify me. And one day they did.

I was invited to perform a spoken-word poem at a conference, and I had said yes.

The only woman on the conference's bill, I was prepared that some might question if my presence should be allowed, knowing the varying viewpoints on women's roles in ministry.

I love when the church comes together, listens to one another, and learns together. It's a beautiful thing. And though no gathering of people will ever be on the same page about everything, with the common goal being to glorify Jesus as best as we can, especially among groups within the local and global church, I know we can have awesome, God-honoring conversations about all sorts of things. I have them with friends of varied perspectives all the time.

So though I expected questions, and maybe even further discussion, I was not prepared for the aggressive, hurtful ways people would speak about me across the internet. I was not prepared for other Jesus-followers who went beyond voicing their disagreement to being mean and degrading toward my gender and race. I was not prepared—at all.

I read posts on social media from people making racist plays on my last name, Wong, a name I had once tried to hide by going by "Hosanna Poetry" in fear that one day it *would* be made fun of. I read all sorts of hurtful things I don't really want to repeat, but many were iterations of: she's not "white" enough for this event and she's not white; she's wong.

Not clever. And not okay.

I saw posts, tweets, and comments calling me names and telling me to please *go home.*

I read of groups of people who threatened to boycott the event if I remained invited. I read their threats to my safety if I showed up. I saw photos of a PowerPoint of all the reasons I was unqualified. (Years earlier I had actually made the same list, and, frankly, they had left out a few things.)

The fears I once had as a young girl came to pass.

Every insecurity I had fought to be free from: *I'm not the right gender. I'm not the right race. My story isn't the right story. I'm not the right person.* All these things had once stood in the way of me confidently obeying what God called me to do, and now I watched as other Jesus-followers used them against me.

I wasn't able to read their protests for long. Quickly my phone was flooded with texts and calls from my mentors, friends, and heroes: "Turn off the internet." Choosing to listen to them was the best decision my husband and I could have made. I love our people. They had been through similar trials countless times and wanted to make sure we weren't alone or unprepared.

Still, I couldn't unsee it. Everything I thought would disqualify me, there it was for anyone to see and anyone to weigh in on.

And once again I got a visit from my old friend: guilt.

Guilt as staff members from my church had to field phone calls and emails asking for statements. Guilt as my mom called in tears as she read things posted online before I got to tell her about them. Guilt as I had to explain to my nieces, the two most ambitious mixed-race Chinese, Filipino, and Mexican girls I've ever met, who have never imagined that they couldn't do one thing, why some people were saying these things about their auntie. Guilt as my friends, who did not yet have a personal relationship with Jesus, were calling me, confused and angry, with so many questions, and yet rushing to comfort me at the same time. *Jesus, help us be better examples to those who don't know You.* Guilt as my baby brother, Elijah, who had just accepted Jesus into his life a few months before, called and said, "You know I believe in you, right?" I listened as someone I once fought for was now fighting for me. I felt terrible.

I thought to myself, *I knew I shouldn't have started preaching. I knew I shouldn't have started going by* Wong. *I knew this would happen. What was I thinking?*

I had to call back to mind what I had learned years before.

Staring in my bathroom mirror, wiping tears streaming from eyes that I had once hated but have now grown to love, I had to remind myself:

I am not less than. I am not second-rate.

I was made in the image of God.

Value runs through my veins. Dignity is in my DNA.

I serve a Savior who elevated those the world saw as outcasts and
   unlikely.

Who accepted Mary as His disciple as she sat at His feet.

Who ate meals with Zacchaeus. With Matthew. With
   everybody.

Who spoke to the Samaritan woman in the middle of the
   day and changed her life. She told her whole town about
   Him too.

Humans never gave me my value. Humans cannot take it away.

My value comes from God. He put me here. He made me
   this way.

I splashed warm water on my face, washing away my smudged makeup, streaming tears, and self-pity.

I realized that the things people were using against me to tear me down were all things that were not my fault. *These were all traits I was born with.* And I had no part in creating me.

I was born a woman.

I was born Chinese.

I was also born to share the gospel of Jesus.

And so are you.

Whether it is through teaching, writing, mothering children, mothering a church, fathering a congregation, fathering many sons and daughters, coaching, running a business, building furniture, painting houses, or creating art from scratch, you are also born to share the gospel of Jesus through your words and through your life.

Despite what we may disagree on at times, there is a Jesus way to speak to people and a Jesus way to respond. So how will *you* speak to people? How will *you* respond?

What will you do when people tell you that you should not obey what God has called you to do? What will you do when people shout their own qualifications at you as if their credentials are greater than God's? What will you do when people dismiss Jesus' instructions of speaking to people with love and choose instead to speak with intimidation and bullying to tear others down?

What will you do?

Will you quit? Will you throw in the towel and turn your back on God due to the volume of the naysayers and accusers?

Will you stop tutoring the kids God has called you to teach when others tell you that your program will never grow? Will you cease to write songs that God has placed on your heart to write because they may never achieve the amount of sales or streams people have told you makes you "successful"? Will you stop studying to be in the field you felt God called you to—a nurse, a lawyer, a teacher—because of the many telling you you're not smart enough, it's too many years of schooling for you to handle, or it will not have enough payoff in the end?

Will you curl up in defeat?

Or will you grow defensive and think you *must* fight back? Will you write out an articulate rebuttal, a fiery blog post, a list of the reasons you *are* qualified?

Will you yell at those telling you to quit and close the tutoring center? Will you make sure all your next songs are revenge letters about the haters? Will you write long posts on Facebook calling out those by name who told you to quit school and then boast about how you'll "show them"?

Will you take every opportunity to defend yourself, make your anger heard, and cleverly fight back?

David didn't.

BROTHERS AND GIANTS

Young David approached a towering giant named Goliath who was threatening to destroy God's people, and against all odds, he took that giant down. Sling: shot. Stone: soaring through the air. Stone *now*: lodged in Goliath's forehead, causing him to fall facedown to his ultimate demise.

For thousands of years this story has echoed not only in churches and spiritual circles but also in mainstream movies and everyday sports talk: "This is a classic David-and-Goliath situation. This underdog team is taking the big dogs down!" Even people who don't know Jesus know that a small kid named David once took down a giant named Goliath.

We love this story. It's a good one.

But there was a moment before David walked onto this important battlefield when he had an opportunity to fight a lesser battle. This one was not as public. Still, it had the power to stand in the way of what David was ultimately called to do.

David's dad told him to go to the battlefield (one he was not technically qualified to fight on; he was neither old enough nor a trained solider) to bring his brothers food. While there, he saw how the

Israelites, God's people, were afraid of the opposing Philistine armies, due in large part to the threat of Goliath. No one would stand up to him, so David began asking questions to those around him. "What will be done for the one who takes down this Philistine? Who even is this guy that is defying the armies of the living God?" (1 Sam. 17:26, paraphrase my own. I highly recommend you read 1 Samuel 17 for yourself. It's super good.)

Suddenly, David's brother Eliab stopped him. He was angry that David was even there.

"Why have you come down here? And with whom did you leave those few sheep in the wilderness? I know how conceited you are and how wicked your heart is; you came down only to watch the battle" (1 Sam. 17:28 NIV).

His brother didn't want him there. His brother tried to talk down to him as one who had a less-important role, asking him where his tiny flock was. Then, he insisted the only reason he must be there was because of the sin in David's heart, not considering that he might be there out of obedience, because his father told him to go there.

"'Now what have I done?' said David. 'Can't I even speak?' He then turned away" (vv. 29–30 NIV).

We know how this story goes. ESPN knows how this story goes. David went to the king and said, "Put me in, Coach." (Again, my paraphrase. Pretty good though, right?) He walked onto the battlefield and proclaimed to Goliath: "You come against me with sword and spear and javelin, but I come against you in the name of the LORD Almighty, the God of the armies of Israel, whom you have defied" (v. 45 NIV).

He continued, "All those gathered here will know that it is not by sword or spear that the LORD saves; for the battle is the LORD's, and he will give all of you into our hands" (v. 47 NIV).

David took that giant down.

It's a good thing David didn't stop to fight against his brother Eliab.

It's a good thing David didn't stop to fight for his reputation or defend his ego or prove he was qualified, spending all of his time in a heated argument, and then miss the battle God was actually calling him to.

It's a good thing he didn't say to Eliab, "No, *you're* unqualified; let me make a list of all the reasons why *I should be here* and *you should not*. I'm going to put down my sling and pick up a pen and write out a list!"

It's a good thing David turned away.

I wonder in what ways the Enemy is distracting us from the call of God on our lives because we've decided to settle for lesser battles. I wonder what towering Goliaths are still roaming around in our world because we have chosen instead to take down one another. There are real threats against God's will in our world, in our churches, in our communities, and in our families. Who will take them down? *Who has the time?* Who is not distracted with fighting for their own rank or influence?

Paul wants us to be clear that "we do not wrestle against flesh and blood, but against principalities, against powers, against the rulers of the darkness of this age, against spiritual *hosts* of wickedness in the heavenly *places*" (Eph. 6:12 NKJV).

We are fighting the agendas and advances of the Enemy whose sole purpose is to steal, kill, and destroy God's children.[a] He wants to

---

a. John 10:10 says that the Enemy's sole purpose is to "steal, kill, and destroy" (CEB). That's it. All he wants to do is stand in the way of every good thing God has for you. If you've ever felt like there was someone working against you, you've been right. That's the bad news. The good news is that Jesus is not going down without a fight for your life. He came to give you "life to the fullest"—that's in the same verse. Jesus has come to fight for you to have the fullest peace, the fullest joy, the fullest rest and assurance in His love for you. He loves you too much to stop fighting for you.

steal our joy, kill our confidence, and destroy our relationships. He wants to divide families. He wants to turn children of God against other children of God.[b] He wants to break apart God's church. He wants humans made in the image of God to feel less than, unworthy, and unloved. He wants humans to live without hope and without purpose and to doubt if their lives are even worth living. He wants people to go to their vices, addictions, and spirals of shame before ever going to Jesus. He has an entire plan to take down the people of God one lie at a time.

What battles for people's lives are *you* fighting? What lies are you speaking truth to? What hopelessness are you bringing hope to? Are you fighting the real giants God has called you to fight? Or have there been other battles you have been distracted with?

If we were sitting across a coffee table from each other right now, I would grab your hands and plead with you with all my heart: Friend, don't be distracted. Fighting the wrong battles? That's how (not) to save the world. You do not want to miss the mission God actually has for you.

> **Are you fighting the real giants God has called you to fight?**

When the Enemy cannot completely destroy you, he will settle for distracting you. He will settle for every Eliab in your life who can delay you from stepping onto the battlefield God has called you to. The hateful person on Facebook saying rude things to you whom you spend all your time writing back to. The condescending neighbor who lives next door whom you spend all your energy complaining to your spouse about. The coworker who gets on your

---

b. When Jesus-followers tear down other Jesus-followers it does not entice people to want to follow Jesus. How are we speaking to and about each other in front of a watching world? Belittling and degrading one another is the perfect plan of how (not) to save the world.

last nerve whom you spend all your work hours obsessing over. The last test you got a bad grade on. The last deadline you missed. The last project that you weren't proud of that made you spiral down into a pit of guilt, sitting in muddy feelings of inadequacy for far too long, putting the next project or goal on hold. Whether a discouraging person or a discouraging circumstance, the Enemy loves whenever we dwell in that defeat and stay there. The Enemy loves when we put down our slings, the callings on our lives, the passions welling up inside of us, and instead choose to fight lesser battles.

Do not allow the Enemy to distract you from what you have been put on this earth to do. God has a purpose for your life that is above proving your value to other people, above promoting your own platform, and above fighting against other children of God. In your lifetime you will have the time and capacity to fight some real battles. Which battles will you choose?

REAL GIANTS

In my life I've had many Eliabs, various instances where someone stood against my going where I felt God was calling me to go. My guess is that you have too. My guess is that you've had people tell you that you *couldn't*, you *shouldn't*, or try to slam a door in your face. *God, don't ever let me be the Eliab in someone else's story. I don't ever want to close a door or stand in the way of what You may be calling someone to do.*

Instead, I am reminded of the little girl at eleven years old who committed to opening doors.

That's still the girl I want to be.

At this point, you may expect me to speak against those who

opposed my invitation to the conference and to defend why I think I was right to say yes.

But you won't find that battle.

I am clear about what my battle is.

It's not that I haven't considered trying to prove myself or considered typing out eloquent responses and equally hurtful accusations. It's that I have realized time and time again that the decidedly hurtful people online and offline are frankly not my battle. They are distractions. They are not the adversaries I was created to fight.

There are giants in our midst. Real ones.

Giants of brokenness. Giants of loneliness, addiction, and depression. Giants of racism. Giants of hatred. Giants of gossip and division. Giants of insecurity, physical abuse, verbal abuse, abuse of power, and slavery. Giants of anxiety, hopelessness, and fear. To take these real giants down, giants threatening God's purpose for His people, it's going to take all of us ignoring the temptation to stop at an easier fight and instead live lives fighting the right battles.

I've committed the rest of my life to telling this generation and the next: you can do what God has called you to do and be who God has called you to be. I want you to know that there are battles you have been called to fight, and you have absolutely been created by God and equipped by God to fight them. You were made with intricate design and intention, with God's image on you, for a specific important purpose, for the exact moment that you are living in. Your life is more valuable than you know. Your story is more important than you've ever imagined.

> Your life is more valuable than you know. Your story is more important than you've ever imagined.

God wants to use your life to reveal His love to the people right next to you.

That's a message I am dedicated to sharing for as long as I live.

So people going out of their way to be mean online? They are not my battle.

I am not here to build more walls. I would like to open some doors.

If I want to see souls saved and a generation mobilized for the gospel until the day I die, I don't have time to vindictively respond to bullies on social media. The extra time they have on their hands? I don't have it. I'm busy.

I don't have the time. Neither do you.

What are you busy doing?

Are you busy encouraging your children and the young people in your community to do whatever God has called them to do?

Are you busy volunteering on the hospitality team at your church so newcomers can feel the welcoming love of God when they visit church on Sundays?

Are you busy texting your distant friends and asking how they are? How you can pray for them? If they want to start a virtual Bible study together?

Are you busy going to your friend's soccer games or going to their band's next show?

Are you busy inviting your neighbors over for dinner?

Are you busy raising your kids to be kind and loving?

Are you busy starting the project God put on your heart to start?

Are you busy worshipping God with your words and with your life?

You're too busy for distractions. You're too busy to listen to every voice telling you what you can and can't do. You *literally ain't got no time for that.*

I am *not* saying to never stand up for those being bullied online or to not be a voice for the voiceless in the comment sections or to hold back what you are passionate about in response to anyone.ᶜ Online or offline, I don't know what specific battlefield you're called to or the people you're called to fight for. Just remember that there is a Jesus *way* to speak to people. As you stand up for what you believe in, remember who you represent and who you are speaking to: people created by and loved by God. As long as you are doing it His way, showing His love, I am not dismissing any battle you may be called to.

This is what I *am* saying: With all of your heart and your time and your life, *you must do* what God has called *you* to do. Fight the battles God has called *you* to fight. They may not be the exact same battles as mine. They may differ from your best friend's. They may not be the same as the battles you were called to fight ten years ago. I am saying do not be distracted by each and every battle that comes your way, and don't be distracted by *any* battle, quarrel, or emotion that takes you from the presence of God and from obeying His call on your life.

> With all of your heart and your time and your life, *you must do* what God has called *you* to do.

We do not want to be Christians who masterfully defeat our brothers and sisters on our shared battlefield while the real Enemy, who is out to destroy God's people, roams about and conquers our world. I am not your enemy. You're not mine. I am believing for a unified church that does not fight against one another but fights *for* one another and *with* one another against the darkness that divides and destroys.

---

c. If you're not sure how to reveal God's love online, my guide, "The Truth About Revealing God's Love Through Social Media" in the back of the book is a great place to start!

I HAVE SOMEWHERE TO BE

It's not just about avoiding offensive battles; it's also about avoiding *anything* on your journey that takes your focus and energy from God's call. Sometimes the distraction isn't necessarily evil or bad, it's just that: *a distraction*.

Here's one Jesus avoided.

In Mark 1, we read that Jesus was going from village to village in Galilee, teaching and healing many. Crowds surrounded Him, lines formed around Him (longer than lines for the latest sneaker drop), and many were blessed everywhere He went. In the early morning He went to a solitary place to pray, and His traveling companions tracked Him down, saying, "Everyone is looking for You!" It would seem He needed to go where the demand was. After all, the work He was doing was great work. Instead, He knew He needed to be alone to spend time with His father, to rest and refuel. He replied to those beckoning Him, "Let us go somewhere else—to the nearby villages—so I can preach there also. That is why I have come" (1:37–38 NIV).

Jesus had somewhere to be. Jesus had other things to do. Jesus had some pretty good news that needed to go forth. Yes, there was still ministry to be done where He was, but His time in this specific village had come to an end. Jesus was not deterred by people's preferences. Jesus demonstrates to us: first be found in God's presence, and from that place, live out God's purpose.

Jesus reveals that when we don't spend time with God, listening to what *He is calling us to do*, even a good thing can become a distraction. Even a secure job can be a distraction. Even a growing platform can become a distraction. Even a seemingly effective ministry can be a distraction. We must be aware of the many good things we could do that will distract us from the things we've been called to do. It's not about choosing what seems like the best battle, the most popular battle, or the most lucrative battle. It's also not about choosing the hardest, scariest, most sacrificial battle. It's about spending time with God and asking Him, *What battle do You want me to fight?* And stepping up to the battle God has called you to. There is no other battle worth fighting. No other human is worth following. No hero nor naysayer is worth all your attention, devotion, or praise. No battle is more important than the battle God has put in front of you.

At the end of our lives, when we see Jesus face-to-face, we will not be held accountable for what others told us to do and not do. We will only be held accountable for what God said to do and if we did it. You have been designed in God's image for God's purposes, and you are equipped and empowered to do everything God has called you to do. So I hope you do it.

What do you do when God calls you to do something but other people disagree?

Do what God calls you to do.

What do you do when God calls you to do something but the task seems too daunting?

Do what God calls you to do.

What do you do when God calls you to do something but there are so many other distractions pulling you left and right?

Take command of your focus. And do what God calls you to do.

For the glory of God and the saving of souls:

Will you choose to serve Jesus and not serve the opinions of people?

Will you choose to build God's kingdom and not yours?

Will you choose to not settle for lesser battles but, instead, spend intentional time with God, asking, *What have You called me to do?*

What have You called me to say? What battles have You called me to fight?

Will you shut out the lies and be who you are created to be and do what you are created to do?

Will you listen to God's voice above any other voice?

Will you obey God above anyone else?

When we do, the agendas of the Enemy are canceled, and the giants of our world will fall to their faces in defeat.

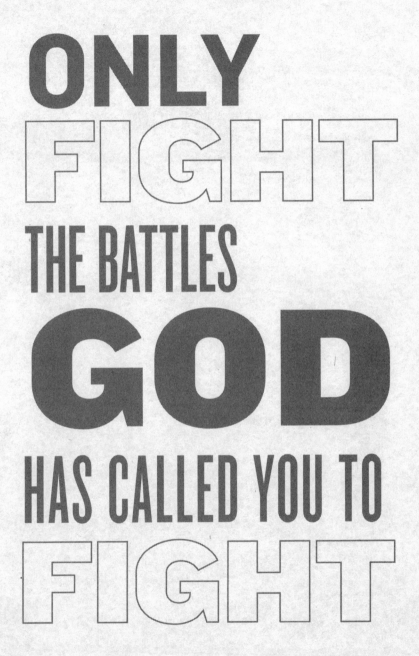

ONLY FIGHT THE BATTLES GOD HAS CALLED YOU TO FIGHT

A Piece on Identity: "I Have a New Name"

Watch a live performance of this spoken-word piece at:
hosannawong.com/interludes

God spends a lot of time in the
    Bible
Telling us who we are
It's almost as if He knew that we
    would doubt
Who that was from time to time
It's as if He saw it coming
That we'd spend our whole lives
    searching
For what our identity—what our
    real name was
And that there'd be many
    moments in our lives
Where we'd let different kinds of
    names define us

When we've looked in the mirror
Compared ourselves to pictures
And heard the name, Ugly

When we've been left by loved
    ones
People we trusted once
And heard the name, Unworthy

When we've been drowning in
    discouragement
Living in a seemingly never-
    ending crisis
And heard the name, Forgotten

When we've had our hopes up
    and our hearts open
Only to be brought down by
    closed doors
And we've heard, Rejected

When we've looked for infinite,
    affirming love
Through lesser, physical, fleshly
    versions
When we gave it away or when it
    was stolen
And we heard, Impure, we heard,
    Garbage

When we go to other vices to
    ease our pain
And we hear, Addict, we hear,
    Forever Broken

When we feel like we're living in
the shadow of someone else's
calling
And we hear, Second Place

When our pain cripples us to a
point where we don't even
know how to let others in
And we hear, Lonely

When our past seems too gross
for others to forgive
And we hear, Disgusting

It's overwhelming—these voices
we're constantly hearing
It's suffocating—this air of
constant critique and
comparing
And it's sort of amazing—the
people whose voices I've
allowed to name me
The power I've given to my
past, to my mirror, and to my
surroundings
And enabled them to identify me
The amount of years I've spent
living up to whatever others
say about me

But God says something else
about me
It's like He knew there would be
other voices
So He wrote His voice down in a
timeless
Book of Truths that would remind
us
Over and over again
In the moments when lies would
block His truths
And somehow make us forget

I'm going back to the Source
Not the people I've allowed to
represent God to me
But the actual, literal, tangible
words that He has written
down for me
And there's some other names
He's given to me

John 15:15—He calls me, Friend

1 Thessalonians 1:4—He calls me,
Chosen

Ephesians 2:10—He calls me, *His
Masterpiece*

He calls me His art, He calls me
handmade
He calls me purposed and
fashioned for good things

1 Corinthians 6:19—He calls my
body, A Temple
He calls it the residence of the
Holy Spirit

Acts 1:8—He calls me, His
Messenger to the World

Galatians 3:26—He calls me, His
Child

Romans 5:8—He calls me, Greatly
Loved

John 8:36—He calls me, Free,
Free Indeed

2 Corinthians 5:17—He calls me,
Brand New

And it's amazing how different
these names are from the
names I'm used to listening to
And in my journey to discover
who I really am

In my battle to uncover the truths
of myself
I've learned something new
about my name, and now this
is what I am certain of

My name is not the name the
world calls me
My name is not the name my past
calls me
My name is not even the name my
own mirror calls me
But my name is the name I
answer to

And I can choose today
From this moment forward
To answer to a new name

When I hear, Lonely
That's not me
When I hear, Disgusting
That's not me
When I hear, Unworthy
I don't even look over my
shoulder
When I hear, Broken
They must have confused me—
please, look elsewhere

When I hear, Ugly, Abandoned,
    Useless, Forgotten
I figure someone just has to
    remind them
Maybe those were my old names
But they're no longer the names
    that I respond to
My name is the name I've chosen
    to spend my days living up to

And if these other voices
Are not saying the same thing
    that the Truth is
I look in my mirror and I
    repeat this:
"They have no right to be
    speaking to you"
When you stop answering to your
    old names
They stop having power over you

The names that my Father
Eternity's Author
The world's Creator has called me
Are the only names that I answer
    to

When I hear, Friend of God—
    that's my name
Chosen—that's my name

Loved, Wanted, Created with a
    Purpose—that's my name
God's Temple—that's my name
God's Messenger—that's my
    name

Child of God—you must be
    looking for me
Greatly Loved—you must be
    calling for me
Brand New—that is my name,
    that is the name that I respond
    to

The Enemy has no power here
Perfect Love casts out fear
And Perfect Love has named me
    and you

So what is your new name
What is stirring up inside of you
When you hear these words, that
    His Word, that the Word has
    proclaimed
What do you know is the name
    God is calling you

Maybe it's not the name you grew
    up with

Maybe it's not the name your old
friends associate you with
Maybe it's not the name that your
whole life you were used to
identifying with
But it's the name you now answer
to
So when the Enemy tries to get
to you

It's the name you introduce
yourself with
As for me, my name is Forgiven,
my name is Free, my name is
Brand New
Loved, Wanted, Child of God
Created with a Purpose
And it's been a pleasure to meet
you[1]

How (not) to Save the World

#14 | Never Take a Breath

I met the man of my dreams and almost ruined our marriage by the end of our honeymoon.

We met three years before. He was a worship leader in Las Vegas at a church that was bringing me in to perform spoken word at an event. (To be clear he's not the one who hired me—this wasn't the cliché book-the-touring-nomadic-poet-to-put-a-ring-on-it situation. *Classic.*) We dated long distance as I continued to travel and minister full time around the country, until we tied the knot in a backyard overlooking my hometown. Since our entire dating relationship was long distance, he had no way to know what it would be like to have two weeks off to be together—the week of our wedding and the week of our honeymoon. Much to his surprise, I didn't know I was *supposed* to take those weeks off.

So I didn't.

I preached at a conference in Ohio a couple days before our

wedding in California. I assured him, "I'll make it in time for the rehearsal dinner, don't worry." And I did. Barely.

I also didn't take one day of our honeymoon completely off. I was working on an upcoming spoken-word album, had phone meetings with a couple of graphic designers, and was emailing back and forth with the coordinators of upcoming events. Even as we embraced above cascading green hills while soaring in a vibrant rainbow-colored hot air balloon, ate delicious meals garnished with decadent dark-chocolate desserts, and visited Tuscan-style castles with hand-chiseled stones now converted to restaurants and outdoor courtyards, I never stopped talking about work and my endless to-do list that I had to tackle when we got back home—or back to our hotel room that night.

Yes, he stayed married to me, but, you know, *pray for him*.

We were surrounded by beauty and . . . I missed it. This was the week most little girls dream about when they are growing up. And me? I was too busy for it. What's worse? I didn't even realize that what I was doing wasn't working. I figured this was different. A career of vocational ministry was a noble cause, right? This didn't really count as work!

It did.

For the next few months he didn't bring it up. We were newly married, and he wasn't sure *how* to bring it up, even as I continuously proved I had no idea how to have relationships while having this career. In fact, one time we crossed paths outside our apartment as he was on his way home from work and I was leaving to go to the airport. He saw my suitcases and said, "Hey, sweetheart, where are you going?" I replied, "I'll be in Kansas and Missouri for two weeks. I'm doing a mini tour there. See you soon!"

When I returned from that tour he kindly asked if I would let him know in advance when I would be gone for two weeks. I felt like that was fairly reasonable, and we never spoke about it again.

I've spent a lot of my life finding my identity in my productivity. The busier I was, the more successful I felt. In fact, I'll just raise my hand and be blatantly honest since you and I are so well acquainted at this point: I've made the effectiveness and efficiency of my ministry an idol, and I've traded being *with* God and being *with* people for being a fast-paced machine producing *for* God and *for* people. In pursuit of the mission of Jesus, I've often neglected spending time with Jesus and His people, missing the mission completely.

I was so wrong.

Never taking a breath? That's how (not) to save the world because it's the opposite of the full, abundant life Jesus came to give us.

From Jesus we learn a rhythm of resting and a lifestyle of retreating and drawing closer to God. We have story after story of Jesus resting, praying, and spending time alone with God,[a] even when others were eager for His time, and we have stacks of stories of Jesus eating with and enjoying time with His friends.[b]

Jesus invites us to live like Him and to remember who follows whom. "I have set you an example that you should do as I have done for you. Very truly I tell you, no servant is greater than his master, nor is a messenger greater than the one who sent him" (John 13:15–16 NIV).

When we see the example of the life and rhythms of Jesus and

---

a. Luke 5:15–16: "Yet the news about him spread all the more, so that crowds of people came to hear him and to be healed of their sicknesses. But Jesus often withdrew to lonely places and prayed" (NIV). There was a lot of work to be done, and yet Jesus made it a priority to leave the crowds and spend time alone with God. I'm amazed by that. I want to do more of that. Here are a few more verses of Jesus praying and resting, just for fun: Matt. 26:36; Luke 6:12; 9:28; 11:1.

b. One of my favorites! "Not long after, Jesus and His disciples traveled to the Judean countryside where they could enjoy one another's company" (John 3:22). In the midst of His mission, the Savior of the world also made a point to hang out with His friends.

we ignore it, is it because we think we are greater than Him? Do we think we need to outdo Him? Do we feel we need to work harder than Him? Do we think He punched out on His timecard too frequently? Do we think, perhaps, if Jesus didn't rest as much, His life could have been more effective?

ZION

I think back to my childhood and about how hard my family worked on mission for God. Immersed in ministry, and with a deep conviction to see the lost saved on the streets of San Francisco, my dad was for sure a powerful force to be reckoned with. He also rarely took intentional time off.

Hopefully by this point you know how much I adore my late father. He ignited a fire in me to preach the gospel and to love those far from God who I will never take for granted. He loved my mom and loved us kids so very much, and it was his greatest joy to serve Jesus alongside of his family. My dad was a great parent. But I don't know if he knew how to be a child—God's child, loved and valued, even if he didn't accomplish one task. I don't know if he knew he was allowed to retreat, to be filled up by God, not just pour out for God, and he didn't need to live with the burdens of the entire city's salvation on his shoulders. It was noble work indeed. We would share the gospel on the streets, rain or shine, sick or well. I didn't know anything else, and I truly loved serving Jesus alongside my family.

Still, we did not take full days off together and never took family trips or went on vacations designated solely for rest and quality time with one another. Once a year, typically the first week of August, we would drive to Twain Harte, a town outside of Yosemite, for about five days. A small town in the forest, with cowboys riding on horses alongside of us on the way to the grocery store, was a fun time for us kids for sure. My dad would preach at a church there and meet with people throughout the week. We'd also talk about our ministry plans for the upcoming year throughout our meals, and fun times playing mini golf and swimming at the lake were infused into all of it! This was our yearly Sabbath. Others took their Sabbath once a week; we did it once a year.[c] This is likely why I thought vacations were only earned if they were centered around work at least 80 percent of the time and why I didn't take time off work for my honeymoon. I didn't know that some trips were *only* for rest, not just infused with *some* rest. It was not until I married my husband that I learned something was off.

Almost a year into our marriage, Guy and I started traveling together. We were in the middle of a six-month tour, driving from Idaho to Arizona, when we discovered we had an extra day between events. What a treat! He suggested we stop in Utah, stay the night, go exploring together, and finish the drive the next day. I protested that if we hyped up on caffeine and drove through the night, we could get to our destination a day early, and we could use that extra day to do some extra work and get a head start on future projects. *What fun, right?* I know, I'm a joy.

My husband said to me, "Hosanna, you're a really hard worker. And that's amazing. I know you work really hard for God. But I don't know if you *enjoy* God."

Whoa! Wait a second. What was this crazy man talking about? How are people going to get saved if I just sit back and enjoy God?

But deep down, his words felt like a punch to the gut, and I had a sneaky suspicion they might just be true.

---

c. Clearly, ours was the wrong approach.

He continued, "Look up how far Zion National Park is. We're going to drive there, stay the night, go hiking, and take tomorrow off to enjoy God, each other, and the world He's made for us."

The next day we hiked the 1,488-foot-tall rock formation called Angels Landing. We were surrounded by mountainous rocks of various golden hues and covered by a perfect periwinkle sky that began collecting small clouds throughout our hike. The sunny but surprisingly chilly weather welcomed us the whole way up. There was hardly anyone around us as we walked uphill, downhill, through boulders, and among rocky cliffs to reach our destination, some sections with metal chains we had to hold tight to in order to navigate the most narrow paths. Once at the top, we felt invincible, the flowing water streams and billowing basil-colored trees beneath us looking like tiny toys far away, a child's board game beneath us.

The small marshmallow-like clouds grew to a darker gray and began to drizzle on my face, eventually intermingling alongside other drops falling from my eyes. The clouds in my heart were beginning to clear. I had dedicated my whole life to helping other people know God, and yet I myself was not indulging in His beautiful world or in the incredible people around me. I almost didn't know how. I knew how to hustle. I knew how to sacrifice. I knew how to be brave. I did not know how to be a child. I did not know how to enjoy God.

> **God cared more about how much time I spent *with* Him than how much I did *for* Him.**

This one hike began a continuous journey of discovering why my identity was found in my productivity and where, along the way, I learned the lie that God cared more about my working for Him than my knowing Him. I had been so wrong. It turns out, God cared more about how much time I spent *with* Him than how much I did *for* Him. In many ways, I'm still on the journey of learning this.

In Genesis 2:8–9, we see the world God originally intended for us, the home He first created for us.

> The Eternal God planted a garden in the east in Eden—*a place of utter delight*—and placed the man whom He had sculpted there. *In this garden,* He made the ground pregnant *with life—bursting forth* with nourishing food and *luxuriant* beauty. *He created* trees, and in the center of this garden *of delights* stood the tree of life and the tree of the knowledge of good and evil.

God first created a playground. He didn't create a church building. He didn't create an office. He created a beautiful, restful, fun-filled, open-aired garden, blooming with color and life.

Why was I spending so much of my life overworking when God originally created the world for us to enjoy it, each other, and Him? Why was I so obsessed with being a hard worker for God and forgetting to rest and take delight in spending time *with Him*?

Why had I spent so many years being a slave to ministry, a slave to productivity, a slave to my checklist, and never fully allowed these words in Galatians 4:7 to change my life: "You are no longer a slave but God's own child" (NLT)?

It's funny, really. I've known this verse most of my life, and whenever I've heard it, I've always basked in the beautiful truth of how Jesus came to set me free from sin, from my past insecurities, from living defined by my hurts. I never once considered the other things—the noble, seemingly good things that I had chosen to be chained to. For those of us who love Jesus and have dedicated our lives to obeying Him and living on mission for Him, if we replace worshipping Jesus the person with worshipping Jesus' mission, we can go from one form of slavery to another. We have been set free from sin, but some of us are so used to being chained that we have now bound ourselves to workaholism or the drive to do as much ministry work as possible, and we are living chained to our accomplishments and newfound checklists instead of living in the freedom of being God's children.

What about you?

- Have you been finding your identity in what you can do for God instead of finding your identity in God?
- Have you been finding your value in how productive you can be?
- Are you exhausted from all the work you're doing at church or all the things you're volunteering for, and trying to hold your breath and brave your way through yet another depleting season?
- Have you chosen to ignore the rhythms of Jesus and make excuse after excuse for why you can't stop and retreat to be alone with God?

When we refuse to rest in God, we are saying that we can accomplish His mission without Him. We are saying we don't need to be filled with His power. We don't need to be found in His presence. We can go forth in our own power. We see ourselves as saviors. We are saying we don't need to be around or connected with His people. We are saying we are better off flying solo.[d]

---

d. If you're not sure where you fall in this dilemma—get real with the people around you. Share, ask, and listen to those who are closest to you. It's worth it. If you're not honest with those you trust and those who love you the most, you may have a seemingly thriving ministry for a period of time without anyone knowing you're spiritually empty, your marriage is hurting, and your soul is broken. God didn't breathe life into us for us to suffocate

It's no wonder that rest is a commandment from God. He knew we would find ways to worship our work, to lose sight of who He is as a Father and see Him only as a boss, and He made sure we knew to rely on Him, trust Him, and rest in Him. He commanded it. While we continue to rush and hustle, saying, "Well, this won't ever get done if I take a day off this month," in various ways God has said: *I command that you rest in Me. I command that you let Me fill you. I command that you let Me show up in ways you've never imagined. I knew you would try to keep going without Me if I didn't command it. How will you know how I can carry you and provide for you if you never let Me? How will you speak on My behalf if you don't even know Me? Why are you trying to accomplish My mission without Me?* [e]

> When we refuse to rest in God, we are saying that we can accomplish His mission without Him.

I am surprised by the words of Paul, which taught me something that goes against every instinct in me: "God chose us to be in a relationship with Him even before He laid out plans for this world" (Eph. 1:4).

We know from plenty of profound prose in Scripture that God has many plans for us—wonderful, life-giving ones! But He chose *first* to be in a relationship with us *before* He made any plans. Many of us choose to skip the relationship and eagerly start all the plans.

The truth is that God wants to know you. He wants you to find

---

ourselves with His mission. Rest is a part of the life He calls us to. Rest also enables us to live out His mission better and more filled. Spending time in the presence of God, revealing the truth of your days to those you trust, is a great way to start taking a breath.

e. Gen. 2:2–3; Ex. 14:14; 20:8–10; 1 Chron. 16:11; Ps. 37:7; 62:1; 127:2; Isa. 40:31; Matt. 11:28–30; Mark 6:31; Eph. 3:20–21; Phil. 4:6–7; Heb. 4:9–11.

your rest, security, joy, and identity in Him. He wants to be close to you. He wants a unique relationship with you.

Then . . . He calls you.

The mission is clear. The people are us. The time is now. But the relationship is first.

THE DREAM OF HAWAII

My dad planned a family trip to Hawaii, and we were shocked. Our family never spent money on anything that wasn't an absolute essential need. We rarely went to restaurants, unless it was my mom's birthday or Mother's Day, when my dad would treat us to Olive Garden or Sizzler. We rarely even ordered takeout pizza, unless it was Super Bowl Sunday, when we would treat ourselves to Pizza Hut stuffed-crust pepperoni pizza—it was a big day! We almost never bought new clothes. All of our cars had always been donated. Most of our food was from the food bank. Honestly, I never felt like we were without, and even now I'm grateful for how I learned to be frugal as a child. Still, trips to Hawaii? Never seemed possible.

Once diagnosed with cancer, my dad was different.

Though we almost never bought new things for our home, and most everything was secondhand, he started buying new things. I'll never forget when we got a new toaster oven. It was so nice. *He bought this—new? What is happening?* He started praying for his grandchildren, praying that he'd meet them, and praying for days with his future family. He had never prayed those prayers before. What was this? Then he booked a family trip to Hawaii. *Who even is he?*

My dad realized it later in life, but he finally discovered that life on earth with Jesus and His people is something to be enjoyed. We are not meant to merely preach abundant life to people; we are also meant to embrace it ourselves. At eighteen years of age, and for the first time in my life, I was going on a real vacation with my family. My dad deeply and sincerely apologized that we had never taken a trip like this before. He promised us no work would be involved, we would get lots of treats, we would eat out, there'd be no preaching at churches or meetings with their staff throughout the week, and we would have uninterrupted time to just be together.

> We are not meant to merely preach abundant life to people; we are also meant to embrace it ourselves.

Two weeks before our trip, my dad went to be with Jesus.

I fell to my knees when I heard the news. I wept uncontrollably at his bedside. Even today I still deeply grieve the loss of one of the best humans I've ever known. And when my mom and I called the airline and hotel to cancel our trip, my heart sank.

For me, Hawaii will always represent the time we missed.

We worked harder than any family I knew. We took less time off than any family I knew. We saw more life change than most do in a lifetime. And yet we missed retreating as a family, trying new things as a family, and enjoying one another outside of ministering together. We missed it. Our trip to Hawaii was two weeks too late.

When I think of the family I hope my husband and I create, I hope we also love Jesus more than anything and love serving Him as a family, just like my parents raised us kids to. But I also have some additional hopes. I hope we don't miss intentional time just enjoying one another. I hope we don't miss taking a breath together. I hope we don't miss resting in the presence of God and enjoying the company of His people. I hope Hawaii happens sooner.

It has taken me a long time to learn this, so please hear this from your sister who is not perfect at this and is still mid-journey in living out these truths. Here is something I have learned: we are called to worship God with our work, but we are not called to worship our work. Ministry is not meant to become your God. It is something we do out of our love for God and others. Ministry is not meant to kill you. Jesus came to save you, not to exhaust you.

It has taken some time, some therapy, and some hard work for me to heal, but on my best days, I live knowing that Jesus is not my job. Jesus is my joy. Jesus is my friend. Jesus is the best thing in my life. I do things out of an abundance of this relationship and joy, but the things I do are secondary to first knowing, loving, and enjoying Him myself.

Out of my job I can get exhausted and treat people as if they're projects. Out of my joy I can bring others the same joy. When I'm filled up by Jesus and excited about who He is and what He does, it's nearly impossible to not spread that joy around. Do not fall more in love with the calling than with the One who called you. Don't obsess over the mission more than the One you're on mission for.

To this day I've never been to Hawaii. I've almost gone a couple of times, but for one reason or another, it's never happened, and the Aloha State remains one of four states I have not yet visited. I know I will go one day. But what it represents to me is far and above what finally going there will ever mean. At the end of my dad's life, he wanted to enjoy God and the ones he loved. When he realized his days were numbered, he was eager to pull out all of the zest of life and cherish every second of it. Later in his life, he began to live this way. I want to live this way now. I want to live in the knowledge that my days are numbered, that life is a fleeting vapor and the people in my life and I are living in a wonderful present that we can enjoy together. We don't want to miss it. We don't want to be two weeks too late for it.

Jesus clarified that "the Sabbath was made to serve us; we weren't made to serve the Sabbath" (Mark 2:27 MSG). Retreating, resting, and refueling with God and His people are made to serve us, fill us, and provide us the abundant life Jesus came to give us. We are invited to rest and enjoy a relationship with God the Father and *also* say yes to what He has called us to do. We can do both. Jesus did both. We are given a beautiful example of doing both, living in abundance as well as living on mission to share that abundance. The lie is that to live on the Jesus mission, we need to live depleted, overwhelmed, and exhausted.

The truth is that Jesus rested, and Jesus saved the world.

Rest in the
ONE
WHO SAVED THE
World

How Jesus Saved the World

(not) A Conclusion

During my dad's last days on earth, his newfound zest for life was on full display. We fit in as many activities together as possible; it was clear his body was growing weaker with each passing day. Still, whenever he would have moments of strength or moments of quick wit and vigorous laughter, he would look to me and say, "Little girl, remember me this way."

My dad wanted to be remembered at his best. At his strongest. He wanted to make sure that when I wrote a book one day and described him in detail, I would make him look really, super good. (That's a joke. Sort of.) My dad had an idea of how he wanted to be remembered and how he hoped we would speak of him long after he passed.

As I sit at my chipped dark-wood dining room table today, typing these final words and recalling the man he was, I don't remember my dad as sick or weak or frail. Instead, I remember my dad as a man who, throughout my childhood, led hundreds of men and women to Jesus. I remember my dad as a man who, whenever he could, would play basketball with all the young men, gang members, and runaways in our neighborhood. They would always say to him, "Hey, old pastor man, if you can sink more free throws than us, we'll go to church with you!" So I remember my dad shooting free throws . . . a lot. He'd spend hours practicing them and later showing up those punks! I remember him bringing them to church with us and saying to them, "I guess you got to work on your game, little boys." (Clearly, basketball ministry is a whole other thing.)

I remember my dad as a man who would step up to the boys who wanted to date me in high school and say to them, "Hey, little man, I wasn't *always* saved, and I am *barely* saved now, so you better watch yourself with my little girl." (So strange that none of those relationships worked out.)

I remember my dad at his best. At his strongest. That's how he wanted to be remembered. That's how I want to describe him to all of you. I can still hear his voice clearly in my head: *Remember me this way.*

AT THE TABLE

The words "Remember me this way" come to mind whenever I think of Jesus' final days on earth. The night before He died on the cross for all of our sins and fulfilled His mission on earth, He sat at a table with His friends, His disciples. He ate with them, shared wine and bread with them, and then said, "Do this in remembrance of me" (1 Cor. 11:24 NIV).

When I think of Jesus at this table with His friends, I can't help but think that Jesus was hours away from being beaten, left naked, alone, and crucified. And yet, *in community*, He showed them how He wanted to be remembered. In candlelight, with the aroma of good food and volumes of lively conversation filling the air, He showed them the picture He wanted them to remember when they spoke of Him after He left.

Remember me this way.

I can't help but remember who was at that table that day.

Judas was at that table.

Judas lived life closely with Jesus, served Him, traveled with Him, did chores with Him, walked far distances with Him, shared sacred moments with Him, and yet was about to betray Him for thirty pieces of silver. And still Jesus sat at that table with him. Judas was present in the picture Jesus was painting for everyone, the story Jesus knew would be told for thousands of years. Jesus sat there with Judas.

Remember me this way.

Peter was at that table.

Peter was the guy who trusted Jesus so much that he walked on water to follow Him. Peter ended up doubting Jesus and almost drowning, soaking wet in the ice-cold sea, but Jesus saved him. They had so many adventures together. They stayed up late and shared stories together. They had a close friendship, a brotherhood. Jesus even told Peter that he would be the one on which the church—the one and only bride of Christ, yes, *that church*—would be built. And yet Peter was hours away from denying he even knew Jesus. Three times.

Jesus knew that. Still, Jesus sat with him. Still, Jesus was in community with him, eating with him and chatting with him.

Remember me this way.

Jesus gave us a vivid memory of how He wanted to be remembered. He gave it to His disciples at that table and to the disciples who would come after His death. We honor this through the beautiful, sacred tradition of communion. By taking the juice or wine, we remember the blood that Jesus shed for us, His blood that covers us and redeems us from all of our sins, all of our shame, and all of our brokenness. By taking the bread, we remember that Jesus' body was broken for us. We no longer have to pay the price for anything we've done against Him, and we are free to have a relationship with God.

By coming together *in community*, we remember Jesus at His best. We remember Him at His strongest. Jesus sat with people who didn't love Him like He loved them and didn't respect Him like He respected them. That's how He wanted to be remembered, not alone, but at a table, in community with all different kinds of people.

I believe Jesus wants *us* to be remembered this way as well. All of us who have chosen to follow Him, all of us who love Him, and all of us on a mission to make His name known. I think He wants His church to be remembered *in*, *with*, and *for* community. It would be a grave disservice to you and to the kingdom of God if you finished this book and felt fired up to try to out-minister other people. This mission is meant to be done in unity, arm in arm with other Jesus-followers. In community, we are our best. Linked together, we are at our strongest.

To partner with Jesus on His mission, here are some things we must do:

- We must resist division. Instead of slamming doors, facilitating factions, and creating cliques, we need to surrender our pride, call that person we hurt, and apologize.
- We must resist comparison and jealousy. We need to vocally cheer on one another and pray that our brothers and sisters succeed and flourish in what God has called them to do.
- We must resist gossip. We need to stop ourselves before spreading hurtful stories, and we need to opt out of social groups that focus on speaking ill of other people rather than building others up.

- We must resist competition within our communities. We need to resource one another, partner with one another, and seek to strengthen one another, because when one of us furthers the mission, it's a victory for all of us. It's a victory for Jesus. It's a victory for the mission at large.

- We must resist the temptation to make the mission all about building our own kingdoms instead of the kingdom of God. We must continuously come to an honest place of surrender, asking God, "Is this glorifying You or glorifying me?"

It's time for we the church to get real. To get real with ourselves, to get real with God, to get real with others, and to get real about the mission God has called us to. No more *playing church*. No more *playing community*. No more preaching amazing love without practicing actual love. It is time for us to fall back in love with the person of Jesus and fall back in love with His people. It's time to be who we were created to be and live as we have been called to live.

GOING TOGETHER

In the final hours of Jesus' life, He reminded us of our mission. He did not choose to fight *against* the people at that table. His mission was to fight *for* them. He did not waste time fighting a lesser battle. He had to save us from all our sins. He did not say, "I have a list of things I'd like to say to you to make you feel guilty, shameful, and less than, so I'm going to sit here for a few hours and fight against you." No, He was called to a greater battle. Instead, His actions said, "See you tomorrow. I'll be at the cross, fighting *for* you."

His mission was to fight for people. May we remember Him that way. May we go and do likewise.

May they remember *us* this way. Sitting at tables it may be hard to sit at.

May they remember us this way. Fighting for people it might be hard to fight for.

May they remember us this way. Not building up ourselves but building up others. Not worshipping our names but worshipping God's. Not telling stories of how amazing we are but telling the story of how amazing Jesus is.

May they remember us at our best. May they remember us at our strongest. May they remember us at a table together, inviting others in.

Friend, I am sorry for the lies you have been told of what it will take to save the world. I am sorry you have been told to rely on your own power, that you have to do something big to do something impactful, that your story should be silenced, that you can do it all alone, and that you never need to take a breath. I am sorry for every way the Enemy has used the mission of Jesus to scare you, guilt you, or deplete you instead of free you and fuel you.

Live in this truth today: Jesus has already saved the world.

His invitation is first to know Him and *then* to partner with Him on His mission for others to know Him too. You have been created and equipped for that very mission, in your lifetime, with your details, your personality, your passions, your position, and your real, authentic relationships.

The greatest work has been finished. Sin has a conclusion. Death has been ended. Jesus has already saved the world.

But His mission is not finished.

This is where you and I come in.

This is not a conclusion.

This is a commission.

We are His chosen plan to make sure everyone knows they are invited. We *can* tell all our friends. We *can* let His joy seep through our lives. You and me giving invitations, having conversations, and sharing our stories *will* reveal God's love to the people right next to us. Everything depends on people knowing how good God is. Every life needs to know about how freeing Jesus is. Every person needs to know how loved and valued they are by God. And each and every one of us has been equipped to be a part of this exact mission—the most important mission in the world. The most exciting news anyone can ever say and anyone can ever find out. We have everything we need to share it. All we must do is say yes.

Will you say yes?

Will you remember Jesus at His best and strive to live like Him? Serving people more than impressing them? Hanging out with people you don't understand yet or may not fully agree with? Sitting at tables with people, even when it's hard? Fighting for people who aren't fighting for you? Enjoying the company of God and the company of others?

Will you join Jesus on His mission to set other people free?

I hope you do.

I look forward to being on this mission alongside of you. Eating the best meals, taking some big steps of faith, fumbling here and there but being rescued through it all. Going to art festivals, reading comic books, having more random but life-giving relationships than we've ever imagined, and sharing the hope of Jesus with those right next to us.

Together.

Sharing all of our stories.

Sitting at all the tables.

Opening all the doors.

THANK YOU

Guy. One of my favorite parts of writing this book was texting you my favorite quote from each chapter as soon as I finished it. You always made me feel like it was the best thing you had ever read. You're amazing and hilarious for that. Thank you for encouraging me every step of the way. Thank you that as we lead together and build together, you always make it fun together. My partner. My love. Life alongside of you is one of the greatest privileges and joys of my lifetime.

Mom, Elijah, Candace, Adonis, Eden, Gracie, Edmond, and Judah. I love you, family. Thank you for allowing me to share so much of our story and so much of Dad's story. Oh, the amazing things we've seen God do on the corner of Jones and Eddy and all throughout our city. I love you all so very much.

My friends on the streets in the Tenderloin district in San Francisco. My family. I wouldn't be who I am without you. I love you with all my heart.

Sean, Shelley, Allison, Kate, and Emily. Thank you for opening your door for me. You changed my life. I'll never be the same. I love you, family.

Bill, Sue, Samantha, Lance, Amelia, and James. Thanks for

welcoming me into your family and teaching me all the card games. Can't wait for our next tournament. I love you all.

Chris and Rachel. Thanks for inviting me to perform at your camp all those years ago and for encouraging me to do something different. I wouldn't be where I am without you. I love you guys.

Natalie. My ride or die. Thanks for sticking with me, standing by me, and always reminding me who I am. I'm a better woman because of you. Music videos and chips and queso forever. You're amazing. I love you.

Kasey. My sister. For fourteen years you've supported me in every new and weird venture I set out to do. When I was nervous to perform in front of four people at an open mic, you let me rehearse in your apartment and cheered loudly for me every second of the way as if it were the most important moment of my life. Thank you. You're crazy. And I love you.

Jacqui. My girl. I couldn't imagine these past few years without you. I love doing life with you, brainstorming with you, dreaming big dreams with you, and listening to the latest pop music with you. You're one of a kind. And I love you.

Jud and Lori. Thank you for who you are and how you fight for people. Thank you for being two of my best friends, teachers, and confidants. I don't know where I would be without you. Thanks for how you encourage me to be exactly who God has created me to be. I love you guys.

David and Lisa. Thank you for how much you've encouraged me and stood by me through thick and thin. I wouldn't have the boldness to write some of these words without you. I love you.

Christine. Thank you for paving the road. Thank you for your friendship, your leadership, and for challenging and encouraging me to unashamedly say all God has called me to say and do all God has put on my heart to do. My friend and my hero, I love you so very much.

Shelley, Lisa B., Priscilla, Laurie, Victoria, Lisa H., Bianca, Jamie, and Rebekah. Without your friendship, encouragement, and words of wisdom, I don't know where I would be. I love you all with all my heart. Thanks for how you fight for people, how you welcome people, and how you love people. What a joy to serve this generation together.

Lysa, Joel, and Shae. Thank you for being the first to read this book, for encouraging me, and for pushing me to write bolder than I've ever written before. This message wouldn't be what it is today without you. Thank you.

Bethany, Elaine, Ali, Bryce, Dustin, Marla, Brandi, Laura, Margaret, Allison, Lindsay, Shauna, and Rachel. Thank you for years of friendship and for riding with me through the thick of it. For real. I love you.

James, Rebecca, Mike, Carmen, Kevin, Patriece, and the amazing church family at EastLake Church and throughout the Community Church Movement network. Thank you for your leadership and friendship. I am so grateful to this community. I honor you and love you all very much.

John, Cheryl, Johnny, Jeni, Mac, Mary, Marnie, and the entire Celebrate Recovery forever family. I wouldn't be the woman I am today without all of you. I am so grateful for all you've taught me. I love you all. We miss you, John.

The entire Central Christian Church family. I love you guys. Thanks for years of friendship and support.

Jonathan. This book wouldn't be what it is without you. Thank you for believing in this message and pushing me to write with conviction and authority. I'm so grateful for you.

Jenni. Thanks for believing in the message of this book. An immense joy to work with you and dream with you.

Jaimie, Whitney, Kristin, and my ministry team. This was a massive endeavor! Thanks for joining me on this mission. I'm so grateful and love each of you very much!

My entire team at W Publishing and Thomas Nelson: Damon, Debbie, Dawn, Stephanie, Laura, Allison, and Caren. The mission is clear. The people are us. The time is now. What a joy to mobilize a generation for the gospel together. We were the team to do this project together! And I am forever grateful for how much you believed in this message, fought for it, and supported it. I love you, team!

Every pastor, church, event, conference, and ministry that has invited me to share about Jesus with your communities. Thank you for your trust and for your friendship. What a joy it is to partner together, love people together, and make Jesus known together.

Finally, thank you—to Mrs. Lee and to anyone who has ever opened a door. You will never know the lives you have impacted for forever. With all my heart, thank you.

The Truth About Revealing God's Love Through Social Media

A Guide

We have bought into a dangerous lie if we believe our words on social media don't matter. The truth is that there is power in every word we speak *and* every word we type. In every post, in every comment, in every private message, our words have the power to bring life or death (Prov. 18:21), the power to wound (Prov. 15:4), and the power to heal (Prov. 12:18).

So how are we choosing to use our power?

It can be all too easy to slip into surefire ways that divide and damage, cause hurt, and stir up hate. In fact, the Bible is pretty clear about how *not* to reveal God's love on social media.

1. **Use your words to tear down.** "Don't use foul or abusive language. Let everything you say be good and helpful, so that your words will be an encouragement to those who hear them" (Eph. 4:29 NLT).

2. **Post, comment, and share as if your digital words don't matter.** "And I tell you this, you must give an account on judgment day

for every idle word you speak. The words you say will either acquit you or condemn you" (Matt. 12:36–37 NLT).

3. **Speak to others solely based on how they speak to you.** "When we are slandered, we respond graciously" (1 Cor. 4:13 CSB).

It turns out, there is a better way: "Don't copy the behavior and customs of this world, but let God transform you into a new person by changing the way you think. Then you will learn to know God's will for you, which is good and pleasing and perfect" (Rom. 12:2 NLT).

What if we changed the way we approached social media?

What if we saw it through the lens of our calling, as a means for our mission?

Before engaging on social media, consider these questions:

- What has God called you to do?
- What has He called you to say?
- In your lifetime, what do you want to accomplish?
- What tasks has God put on your heart to carry out?

Know the answers to these questions first, then, from that place of calling and conviction, choose how to spend your time on social media—what you want to post and how you want to comment.

Social media is not the goal. But social media can be a tool in which we accomplish our goals, walk in our callings, and carry out the most important mission in the world—to reveal God's love to everyone everywhere.

- If your passion is to disciple young women and lead them to a closer relationship with God, social media can be a place where you write and post life-giving words, practical steps, and scriptures that answer the questions they are asking. This is not for the goal of getting likes but for the purpose of strengthening women. Set aside time in your week to leave encouraging comments on their posts, mourn with them in their losses, and celebrate in their victories.

- If your heart beats for connecting creatives to one another, social media can now be a place where you meet artists, connect artists, and actively have conversations about new projects and the many ways to tell powerful stories.
- If you're called to support people in recovery from addiction, social media can be a place where you stay connected with those you know who are working hard on their recovery. Pray for them with each post they share and continuously message them to check in on them.
- If you are a stay-at-home parent and want to minister to other stay-at-home parents, the internet provides many opportunities to facilitate relationships and connections; to start Zoom Bible studies, prayer groups, and book clubs; and to reach out to other parents and offer them encouragement.
- If you are passionate about encouraging those who are lonely or struggling with depression, social media is a great place to do just that—to reach out and minister to others, offering encouragement and truths from the Word of God, letting them know they are loved and not alone.

THE THREE E'S

A few years ago, in an attempt to reclaim social media as a place of positivity in my life and to discover new ways to minister, I stopped to notice how I spent my time on these platforms. Was I simply scrolling past people's lives, no longer interacting with them? Was I reading heartbreaking posts, saying to myself, *How sad*, and swiping away?

As a personal experiment, I decided to dedicate an entire hour every week to being online with the intention of building people up. I wanted to see how intentionality could change this medium for me. Through these months of being intentional with my time online, I learned three simple practices that were a better use of my time than merely scrolling through posts in my feed. No matter what new apps come and go, there is a Jesus way to approach social media.

I. Engage

It's easy to scroll on our social media platforms and become numb to what people are posting. With so many tiny boxes of colorful updates fighting for our attention, few feel worthy to pause for. We may see people's life updates, baby photos, family losses, and big career moves and begin to resent them, critique them, or compare ourselves to the people posting them—all the while failing to engage with these people as human beings. This does not serve you, and this does not serve them.

Every single person posting is an eternal being who has had fears, hopes, insecurities, losses, and victories. Don't observe people created by God and loved by God as if they're objects to be judged and criticized. Instead, see every person online as someone you can cheer on, make feel seen, and have a life-giving conversation with. Even on social media, you're still called to be Christ's representative, His eyewitness account, His sweet aroma to the world.

2. Encourage

Social media is an opportunity to tell people who they really are. Others on the anti-Jesus mission may want to use their time online to bring people down or make others feel less than, to start hurtful arguments in comment sections or be as mean as possible to those with whom they don't agree. That's how (not) to save the world. Instead, we have the opportunity to build people up by speaking truth to a world saturated with lies. We can interrupt careless scrolling with encouraging scriptures. We can interrupt fear and worry with peace and joy.

While the world is telling people who they're not, we can use social media as a way to tell people who they *are* in Christ. A way to live out your mission on social media is to engage and encourage, even in small ways. Let people know you are with them and for them. Let them know you read their heart-filled post, saw their big accomplishment, and are rooting for them in their new endeavor.

If someone's posts constantly stir up negative emotions in you, feelings of hate, comparison, or not-enoughness, mute them. Unfollow them. Social media does not need to be a place where you feel less than. Instead, let it be a place where you purposefully choose to place value on others and tell people, "You are not alone."

3. Encounter God

One incredible thing social media allows us to see is everybody's prayer requests. This may be through direct prayer requests that they are literally posting, or this may be through what you're *discerning* they may be going through based on what they're posting. Either way, we must not ignore the opportunity to come to God in prayer and fight on someone else's behalf. We can look at our social media feeds as our own daily prayer lists, our own doors into how we can encounter God on behalf of other people.

The internet is not a place where you are exempt from living out the life God has called you to. Through engaging with people, encouraging people, and encountering God on behalf of people, social media becomes so much more than a tool—it becomes a weapon to fight *for* people.

Every method and medium we use should also be used to further the glory of God and the saving of souls. If we're not using social media as a way to tell people they are seen, known, and loved by Jesus, we're doing it wrong.

Don't scroll past the opportunities to mourn with those who are mourning or to rejoice with those who are rejoicing. Don't swipe past the chance to come alongside real people's real-life moments, praying with them in their losses and cheering them on in their wins. Don't miss the open door to reveal God's love to someone on social media today.

I continued the practice of an intentional hour on social media each week for months, and I called it my Hour of Encouragement. I made it a habit to sit outside on my patio, turn on my timer to an hour countdown, and intentionally engage with every post I saw. I encouraged as many people as I could, writing out what I loved about them, missed about them, and how I was cheering for them. I encountered God on behalf of everyone I came across on my feed for that hour, sincerely praying for healing in their lives, hope in their difficult situations, provision for their families, and open doors for their ambitions, careers, and ministries to flourish.

This routine changed me. It led to my heart breaking for what broke other people's hearts, to deeper empathy for those whose posts

I used to just scroll past, to DMs turning into Zoom calls and friendships growing deeper. It led to me not comparing myself to anyone seeming particularly blessed on my feed but instead praying for them to have even more blessings and opportunities.

Those intentional, prayerful hours changed how I saw social media, and these habits are now infused into my online engagement every day. I never want to go back.

I challenge you to try this. If you are on social media every day, I challenge you to spend at least fifteen of those daily minutes dedicated to these three Es. In fact, when you say "Es" out loud it sounds like "ease," which is fitting. This is extremely easy to do, but the results can bring hope and life and spark a sense of joy into other people's lives right where they are. Don't just mindlessly scroll. Don't let hours disappear without purpose. Decide that you will engage with people, encourage people, and encounter God on behalf of people. See those fifteen minutes as an opportunity to use social media as a weapon to fight *for* people, not against people.

THE WHATEVER FILTER

If the mission of our lives is to carry out God's mission, for everyone to be united with Him, then how can we share the truth about Jesus and glorify God through everything we post? How can we be intentional digital ambassadors, revealing God's love online?

We can choose to see everything we post, comment, and type through the lens of our mission and as a way of building God's kingdom here on earth.

One of the things we frequently do before posting our photos online is to put a filter on them. It makes our self-taken, amateur photos look a bit more put together (or like we're wearing flower crowns, a very realistic feature). Philippians 4:8 gives us an even better filter for improving what we put online: "Whatever is true, whatever is noble, whatever is right, whatever is pure, whatever is lovely, whatever is admirable—if anything is excellent or praiseworthy—think about such things" (NIV).

How do we know what to post or comment about on social media? Consider putting this "whatever" filter on it. Is this photo admirable? Is this comment true? Am I living and posting as an example of someone who praises God first and foremost?

- When you try to make your life seem as if it's something it's not, is that right? Is that noble? Put it through this filter. When you choose instead to show your real life, to tell a story that's honest and true, you show how God is truly with us, beside us, and for us, in our imperfect lives. That is something lovely.

- When you comment with something that's condescending and hurtful, is that excellent? Is that praiseworthy? Pause and put your words through this filter. When you choose instead to speak to people with the lens of how much God loves them, that is something noble.

If we are seeking to make ourselves look impressive or to elevate ourselves above other people, then perhaps we're using a different filter entirely. However, if we are living to make Jesus known and for everyone to feel valuable and loved, then the filter in Philippians 4 is a powerful tool to use to make sure we do "whatever" we can for the mission of Jesus.

God can and will use any means to communicate to His people—if we let Him. Social media is an opportunity to be Jesus' witnesses in parts of the world we never imagined we could reach. It can be an effective way to deliver hope, joy, beauty, and truth right into people's hands. It can be a powerful tool to do what God has called us to do and say what He calls us to say. May we carry out His mission both offline and online and through every single way we discover to communicate His love next.

A Personal Social Media Survey

Social media can be a chaotic space, taking up our time and energy and not producing good things within us. But it doesn't have to be. Take an honest look at the minutes and even hours you spend on social media, consider the tools within this guide, and talk to God about how you can best use your time to reveal His love to the people you have connections with.

This short survey, which you might consider taking weekly or monthly, will help reveal your personal habits and challenge you to use social media for good.

1. How do I spend my time on social media? How much of that time is spent judging or comparing? How much is spent connecting and encouraging?
2. Who do I follow, and what kinds of posts do I see that stir up negative feelings and thoughts within me? Is there anyone I need to unfollow today?
3. How have I presented Jesus in what I've posted? How have I presented myself? When I put my past posts through the "whatever" filter, what do I see?
4. How can I engage, encourage, and encounter God through social media this week? When will I do that? What is my plan?

5. What are some ways God might want to use me through my social media channels? In what ways can I use social media to carry out what God has called me to do?

A Prayer Challenge and Five-Step Guide

> When he saw the crowds, he had compassion on
> them because they were confused and helpless, like
> sheep without a shepherd. He said to his disciples,
> "The harvest is great, but the workers are few. So
> pray to the Lord who is in charge of the harvest;
> ask him to send more workers into his fields."
>
> —MATTHEW 9:36–38 (NLT)

There are *many* people who do not yet know how loved and valuable they are to God. *Many* who are unaware of the whole and free life available with Jesus. And yet Jesus said there are *not many* who have gone out to tell them.

In Matthew 9, Jesus told His disciples to pray a specific prayer. Today, as His disciples, we should pray it as well—that God would send more workers, messengers, truth-tellers, Jesus-sharers, and eyewitnesses of who Jesus is and what He can do into the places in our world, our homes, our jobs, and our social circles where people don't know Him. It's a bold prayer, as the disciples discovered—for they were the ones sent out by Jesus in Matthew 10 as the answer to their own prayers.

Are we praying these kinds of bold prayers? I fear that, at times, prayer seems so simple and so obvious it gets ignored altogether. And the Enemy of our souls loves that. The Enemy hopes we see prayer as a passive, powerless practice—religious and spiritual words to the heavens that don't reach the ears of God and certainly are not involved in changing anything here on earth. He hopes we believe that praying for our loved ones won't help anything, *so what's the point?* He hopes that we dismiss the power of prayer so that we don't access the open communication lines we have to God. He hopes we don't pray for more workers to be a part of the harvest. He hopes we give up hope. He wants us to remain silent.

But 1 John 5:14 ensures us that God hears us: "This is the confidence we have in approaching God: that if we ask anything according to his will, he hears us" (NIV).

It is God's will that all should know Him. You are not alone in wanting your loved ones to know God. God loves them even more than you do, and He wants to partner with you in revealing who He is.

I challenge you to crush the Enemy's lie that your prayers don't matter. I challenge you to let your heart break for those far from God, the way Jesus' heart did in Matthew 9. I challenge you to pray as if God hears—because He does. I challenge you to pray like your loved ones can come to know the one true God—because they can. May we be people of faith with actual faith, praying bolder prayers than we ever have.

A FIVE-STEP GUIDE

Colossians 4:2–6 (NIV) gives us a wonderful guide of how to pray not only for those around us who have yet to experience God's love but also for opportunities to reveal it.

1. **Keep praying.** "Devote yourselves to prayer, being watchful and thankful" (v. 2). Don't give up on praying for your loved ones. Live a life devoted to such prayers. This word *devote* in its original Greek form means to consistently show strength, to persist, to persevere, to endure, to keep on.[1] God calls us to persist in prayer. To press on praying with strength. With a thankful heart, be watchful and focus your prayers on the specific needs of your friends and family members. Who will you persevere to keep praying for?

2. **Pray for open doors.** "And pray for us, too, that God may open a door for our message, so that we may proclaim the mystery of Christ, for which I am in chains" (v. 3). Pray to God for opportunities to reveal His love and share His story. God loves opening doors. Pray for them. Look for them. Expect them. And pray for the courage to walk through those doors when they open.

3. **Pray for boldness.** "Pray that I may proclaim it clearly, as I should" (v. 4). Pray for God to give you courage as you share your story and the story of Jesus. And pray that He gives you the right words. Each person you speak to has their own unique lens through which they see themselves, God, and the world. Pray that you are clear in sharing the good news about God's love with them in a way they will receive and understand.

4. **Pray for awareness and wisdom.** "Be wise in the way you act toward outsiders; make the most of every opportunity" (v. 5). Pray that God gives you wisdom in your everyday life. Pray that as you go grocery shopping, go to work, and go to birthday parties God gives you a heightened awareness of the people around you. Pray that your empathy expands. Pray that you are able to make the most of every open door around you.

5. **Pray for gracious words.** "Let your conversation be always full of grace, seasoned with salt, so that you may know how to answer everyone" (v. 6). Pray that as you make invitations and have conversations, your words will be saturated in kindness, your joy will enhance the flavor of people's lives, and the truth you tell of a Savior who rescues and restores will be received for what it truly is: the best news anyone can ever hear. Pray that you listen well. Pray that love leads the way. Pray that through your conversations, God's love will be revealed as the most grace-filled, welcoming, inviting love there is.

Friend, never stop praying. When you don't know how to pray, pray through these verses in Colossians 4. Use it as a guide to pray for your loved ones, to pray for the world, to pray for God to send more workers into His fields and show you how you can be a part of His harvest.

May we pray as Jesus called us to pray. May God open doors. And may we have the courage to walk through them when they open.

NOTES

Chapter 1: Rely on Your Own Power

1. "Upgrade U," featuring Jay-Z, Spotify, track 4 on Beyoncé, *B'Day*, Columbia, 2006.
2. St. Augustine, *Questions on the Gospels by Augustine of Hippo*, trans. John Litteral (Ashland, KY: Litteral Truth Publishing, 2019), 45.

Chapter 3: Check the Easy Box

1. "We Are Never Ever Getting Back Together," written by Taylor Swift, Max Martin, and Shellback.

A Riff on Doubt: "These Waters"

1. Hosanna Wong, "These Waters." Used by permission of the author, hosannawong.com/interludes.

Chapter 4: Wait for Perfect

1. Hosanna Wong, "These Waters." Used by permission of the author, hosannawong.com/interludes.

Chapter 6: Silence Your Story

1. Miles McPherson, *The Third Option* (New York: Howard Books, 2018), 18.
2. Walter L. Liefeld, "Luke," in *Zondervan NIV Bible Commentary*, ed.

Kenneth L. Barker and John Kohlenberger III (Grand Rapids, MI: Zondervan Publishing House, 1994), np.

3. Christopher J. H. Wright, *The Mission of God's People: A Biblical Theology of the Church's Mission* (Grand Rapids, MI: Zondervan Publishing House, 2010), 176.

Chapter 7: Hide Your Faith at Home

1. "One Third of Your Life Is Spent at Work," Gettysburg College, https://www.gettysburg.edu/news/stories?id=79db7b34-630c-4f49-ad32-4ab9ea48e72b&pageTitle=1%2F3+of+your+life+is+spent+at+work.

Chapter 10: Always Fly Solo

1. "Thank U, Next," Spotify, track 11 on Ariana Grande, *Thank U, Next*, Republic Records, 2019.

A Riff on Identity: "I Have a New Name"

1. Hosanna Wong, "I Have a New Name." Used by permission of the author, hosannawong.com/interludes.

A Prayer Challenge and Five-Step Guide

1. Bible Hub, s.v. "proskartereó," Strong's Greek 4342, https://biblehub.com/greek/strongs_4342.htm.

ABOUT THE AUTHOR

Hosanna Wong is an author, speaker, and spoken-word artist who grew up in an urban ministry on the streets of San Francisco. From there to her years of touring the country, sharing Jesus through spoken-word poetry, and on to becoming a sought-after speaker in churches and conferences around the world, Hosanna has learned how to say yes to God no matter how intimidating or uncertain the task. She and her husband, Guy, serve in various ministries, equipping the local and global church. Learn more at www.hosannawong.com.